CONTENTS

This book was approved by Jason Mraz
Cover photo by Bill Zelman

Jason Mraz plays Taylor Guitars

Cherry Lane Music Company
Director of Publications/Project Editor: Mark Phillips

ISBN 978-1-60378-428-3

Copyright © 2012 Cherry Lane Music Company
International Copyright Secured All Rights Reserved

The music, text, design and graphics in this publication are protected by copyright law. Any duplication or transmission,
by any means, electronic, mechanical, photocopying, recording or otherwise, is an infringement of copyright.

Visit our website at www.cherrylaneprint.com

You and I Both

Words and Music by
Jason Mraz

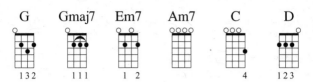

Verse 1

||**G**
Oh, was it you who spoke the words
|**Gmaj7**
That things would happen, but not to me?
|**Em7** |
Oh, things are gonna happen natural - ly.
|**Am7** |
Oh, taking your advice and I'm looking on the bright side
|**C** |**D**
And balancing the, the whole thing.

Verse 2

||**G** |**Gmaj7**
Oh, but at often times those words, they get tangled up in a lines;
|**Em7** |
And the bright lights turn to night,
|**Am7**
Oh, un - til the dawn, it brings
|**Am7** |**C** |**D**
An - other day to sing about the mag - ic that was you and me.

Copyright © 2002 Goo Eyed Music (ASCAP)
International Copyright Secured   All Rights Reserved

Chorus 1

```
                      ‖G                    |Gmaj7
'Cause you and I   both loved
                    |Em7                 |
What you and I      spoke of
                  |Am7                |
And others just      read of.
                |C                    |D
Others on - ly read of, of the love,
                    |G                |Gmaj7
Of the love that I  love,       yeah.
                 |Em7               |
La - ba - da - ba,       yeah.
```

Verse 3

```
                      ‖G
See, I'm all about them words
        |Gmaj7                            |Em7
Over num   -   bers, unencumbered numbered words,
        |Em7                   |Am7
Hundreds of pages, pages, pages for - wards.
         |Am7
More words      than I had ever heard,
C                       |D
   And I  feel so alive.
```

Chorus 2

```
                     ‖G                    |Gmaj7
```
'Cause you and I both loved,
```
                        |Em7                |
```
Uh, what you and I   spoke of
```
                     |Am7
```
And others just   read of.
```
                             |C            D              |
```
And if you could see me now, oh,   love, love.
```
G                          |
```
 You and I, you and I,
```
Gmaj7                         |Em7                    |
```
Not so little, you and I any - more,   mm.
```
       |Am7                              |
```
And a with this silence brings a moral story
```
                       |C                          |D
```
More importantly evolv - ing is the glory of a boy.

Chorus 3

```
                     ‖G                    |Gmaj7
```
'Cause you and I both loved,
```
                        |Em7                |
```
Uh, what you and I   spoke of, of
```
                     |Am7
```
And others just   read of.
```
                         |C
```
And if you could see me now,
```
                        D              |G
```
Well, then I'm almost finally out of,
```
                       |Em7
```
I'm finally out   of,
```
            |Am7
```
Finally di - di - di - di - di - di.
```
                 |C          D           |G                  |
```
Well, I'm al - most finally, fi - nally, well, I   am free.   Oh, I'm free.

4

Bridge

```
               ‖C                    |D
And it's okay     if you had to go a - way.
                    |G                   D
Oh, just remem - ber that telephones,
                                   |Em7
Well, they're workin' 'em both      ways.
           |C                   |D
But if I   never ever hear them     ring,
             |G
If nothing else, I'll think the bells inside
         |Em7
Have finally found you someone else.
            |C            |
And that's    okay
                  |D                          |
'Cause I'll re - member everything you say.
```

Chorus 4

```
               ‖G                      |Gmaj7
'Cause you and I   both  loved,
                   |Em7                |
Uh, what you and I      spoke of, of
                 |Am7
And others just     read of.
                     |C
And if you could see    me now,
                  D                |G
Well, then I'm almost finally out  of,
                 |Em7                 |
I'm finally out      of,
             |Am7
Finally di  -  di - di - di - di - di.
                   |C            D          |G         |              ‖
Well, I'm al - most finally, fi - nally, well, out  of words.
```

I'll Do Anything

Words and Music by
Jason Mraz
Additional Words by
Billy Galewood

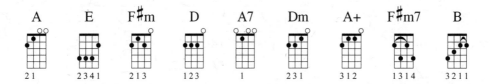

Intro A E |F♯m D |A E |F♯m

Verse 1

         ‖A   E
Go make your next choice, be your best choice.
        |F♯m   D
And if you're looking for a boy with a voice,
        |A   E |F♯m   D |
Well, baby, I'm single.
A   E
Are you in the mood for some dude?
     |F♯m   D
Are you in the mood to be subdued,
         |A   E |F♯m   D
Or would you rather just mingle?
    |A   E
Let's get set then, to go then,
     |F♯m   D
Or let us jet set. We'll be like the Jetsons.
       |A   E |F♯m   D
You can be Jane, my wife. Should I marry Jane to - night?

Chorus 1

      ‖A
See, I would,
    |A7
If I could.
  |D |Dm
I'll do anything sponta - neously.

Copyright © 2002 Goo Eyed Music (ASCAP), Flozkid Music Publishing (ASCAP) and Original Gangster Of Cleveland (ASCAP)
All Rights for Flozkid Music Publishing Administered by Original Gangster Of Cleveland
International Copyright Secured   All Rights Reserved

Verse 2

```
        ‖A                           E
Or we can keep chilling like ice cream filling.
        |F♯m                      D
We can be cool in the gang if you'd rather hang.
        |A           E          |F♯m           D
Ain't no thing. I can be la - cubrious with you.
        |A              E
I got no if, ands, ors, no wits or what's about it.
          |F♯m                              D                    |
But this place is getting crowded and my house is two blocks away,
A      E     |F♯m        D
   Or  maybe    closer.
```

Chorus 2

```
             ‖A
See, I would,

             |A7
Oo, if I could.

           |D              |Dm
I'll do, oh, anything  sponta - neously.

             |A
You know I would,

        |A7
Oh, if I   could.

           |D              |Dm                    ‖
I would do, oh, anything  sponta - neously.
```

Bridge

```
F♯m                     |A+
    If you could be nim  -  ble,
             |F♯m7              |B              |
You'd have it sim   -   ple just like me.
F♯m                |A+
    So go on and try        it,
           |F♯m7            |B      |D          |Dm
Do not deny     yourself your free   -    dom.
```

Verse 3

        ‖**A**   **E**
So step on up to the plate, get a date with Mraz.

       ‖**F♯m**   **D**
See, you better act fast because sup‑plies, they never last.

          A   **E**   **F♯m**   **D**
Now, did you know this is a limited time of ‑ fer?

          A   **E**
So go make your mind up before our time's up.

    F♯m   **D**   **A**   **E**
So you better start winding it up because the party's al ‑ most over.

                 F♯m   **D**
And if you should know, girl,   it's a little bit lower now.

Chorus 3

      ‖**A**
See, I would do,

        A7
Oh, if I could do,

        D   **Dm**
I would do, oh, anything sponta ‑ neously.

        A
You know I would,

        A7
Oh, and I could prove it,

        D   **Dm**   ‖
Oh, that I'll do anything sponta ‑ neously.

The Remedy
(I Won't Worry)

Words and Music by
Graham Edwards, Scott Spock, Lauren Christy and Jason Mraz

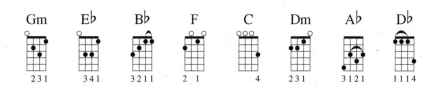

Intro

Gm Eb |Bb F |Bb Eb |Bb F |

Gm Eb |Bb F |Bb Eb |Bb F

Verse 1

        ‖Gm   C
Well, I saw fire - works from the freeway,

      |F   Bb
And behind   closed eyes I can - not make them go away

             |Gm   C
'Cause you were born on the Fourth of Ju - ly, freedom ring.

      |F   Bb
Well, something on the surface, it stings.

             |Gm   C
I said some - thing on the surface, well, it kind of makes me nervous.

         |F   Bb
Who says   that you deserve this, and what kind of God would serve this?

        |Gm   C
We will cure this dirty old disease,

        |F   N.C.
Well, if you've gots the poison, I've gots the remedy.

Copyright © 2002 by Universal Music - MGB Songs, Graham Edwards Songs, Universal Music - Careers, Scott Spock Songs,
Warner-Tamerlane Publishing Corp., Rainbow Fish Publishing and Goo Eyed Music
All Rights for Graham Edwards Songs Administered by Universal Music - MGB Songs
All Rights for Scott Spock Songs Administered by Universal Music - Careers
All Rights for Rainbow Fish Publishing Administered by Warner-Tamerlane Publishing Corp.
International Copyright Secured All Rights Reserved

Pre-Chorus

```
     ‖Gm           C                 |F          B♭
```
The remedy is the experience; this is a dangerous li - aison.
```
              |Gm           C
```
I says, the comedy is that it's serious.
```
              |F              B♭
```
This is a strange enough new play on words.
```
              |Gm                    C
```
I say, the tragedy is how you're gon - na spend
```
              |F                    B♭
```
The rest   of your nights with the light on.
```
              |Gm                  C
```
So shine the light on all of your   friends,
```
              |F  N.C.                       ‖
```
When it all amounts to nothing in the end.

Chorus

```
     B♭      E♭      |
```
I,
```
     F                       |Gm    Dm   |E♭   F      |
```
   I won't worry my life   away.   Hey.   Oh, oh.
```
     B♭      E♭      |
```
I,
```
     F                       |Gm    Dm   |E♭   F      ‖
```
   I won't worry my life   away.   Hey.   Oh, oh.

Interlude   Gm   E♭ |B♭   F |B♭   E♭ |B♭   F N.C.

10

Verse 2

                  ||**Gm**   **C**
Well, I heard two   men talking on the radio
           |**F**   **B♭**
In a cross - fire kind of new reality show.
    |**Gm**   **C**
Un - covering the ways to plan the next big attack.
           |**F**   **B♭**
Well, they were counting down the ways to stab the brother in the…
       |**Gm**   **C**
Be right back   after this, the un - avoidable kiss,
      |**F**   **B♭** |**Gm**
Where the minty fresh death breath is sure to outlast this ca - tastrophe.
     C
Dance with me,
     |**F**   **N.C.**
'Cause if you've gots the poison, I've gots the remedy.

Repeat Pre-Chorus

Repeat Chorus

Bridge

    Gm |**E♭** |
    When I fall in love,   I take my time.
B♭ |**F**   .|
    There's no need to hur - ry when I'm making up my mind.
Gm |**E♭** |
    You can turn off the sun,   but I'm still gonna shine,
B♭ |**F**
    And I'll tell you why.

Pre-Chorus 2

```
        ‖Bb              Eb                    |Ab           Db
Because the remedy is the experience, this is a dangerous li - aison.
         |Bb             Eb
I says, the comedy is that it's serious.
        |Ab              Db
This is a strange enough new play on words.
        |Bb                          Eb
I say, the tragedy is how you're gon - na spend
       |Ab                   Db
The rest   of your nights with the light on.
         |Bb              Eb
So shine the light on all of your   friends,
      |Ab N.C.                            ‖
When it all amounts to nothing in the end.
```

Repeat Chorus

Outro-Chorus

```
        Bb     Eb      |
        I
        F                   |Gm    Dm   |Eb    F      |
          I won't worry my life    away,           no.
        Bb     Eb      |
        I
        F                   |Gm    Dm   |Eb    F    |Bb    ‖
          I won't worry my life    away.   Hey.   Oh,  oh.
```

12

Who Needs Shelter

Words and Music by
Jason Mraz, Chris Keup and Eric Shermerhorn

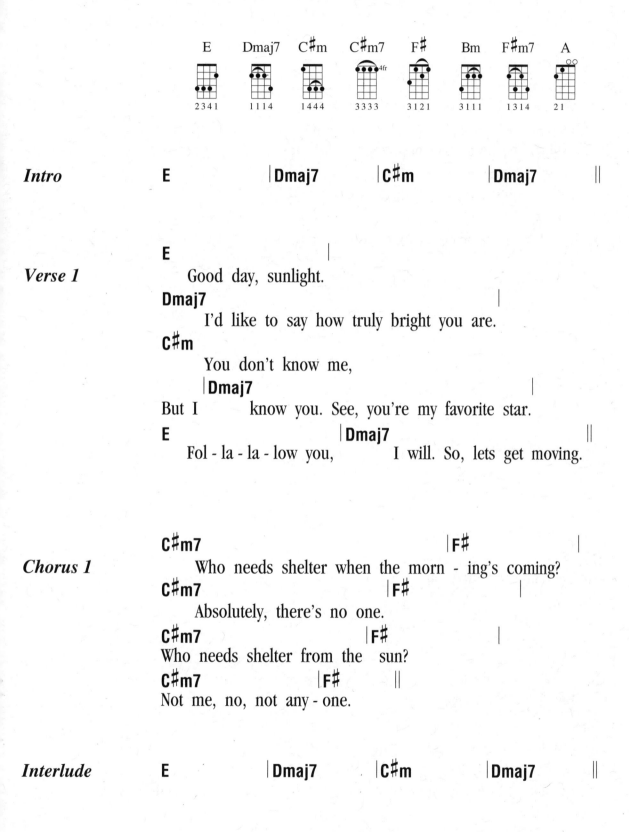

Intro   E |Dmaj7 |C#m |Dmaj7 ||

Verse 1

E |
   Good day, sunlight.
Dmaj7 |
   I'd like to say how truly bright you are.
C#m
   You don't know me,
   |Dmaj7 |
But I   know you. See, you're my favorite star.
E |Dmaj7 ||
   Fol - la - la - low you,   I will. So, lets get moving.

Chorus 1

C#m7 |F# |
   Who needs shelter when the morn - ing's coming?
C#m7 |F# |
   Absolutely, there's no one.
C#m7 |F# |
Who needs shelter from the sun?
C#m7 |F# ||
Not me, no, not any - one.

Interlude   E |Dmaj7 |C#m |Dmaj7 ||

Copyright © 2002 Goo Eyed Music (ASCAP), Stage Three Songs (ASCAP), Grantham Dispatch (ASCAP) and Rocket Seed Music (ASCAP)
All Rights for Stage Three Songs and Grantham Dispatch Administered by BMG Rights Management (US) LLC
All Rights for Rocket Seed Music Administered by Kobalt Music Publishing America, Inc.
International Copyright Secured   All Rights Reserved

Verse 2

```
        E
        By your clock the cock rooster crows,
          |Dmaj7                           |
Then  off to work where everybody goes
        C#m                              |Dmaj7              |
        Slow, but eventually they get          there.
        E
        They're picking up the day shift,
          |Dmaj7
Back          where all left off confined,
          |C#m
And       they're pecking at relationships.
          |Dmaj7                              ||C#m7
You  know,          it's only a worthless piece of shit.
```

Chorus 2

```
                                         |F#              |
Who needs shelter when the morn - ing's coming?
C#m7                            |F#              |
        Absolutely, there's no one.
C#m7                           |F#              |
Who needs shelter from the   sun?
C#m7                    |F#          ||
Not me, no, not any - one.
```

Bridge

```
        Bm            |F#              |
        I'd sleep it all away,
        Bm                   |F#              |
        But the sun won't let  me.
        Bm               |F#        |F#m7    |      A              ||
        I'd miss those lovely days                        of summer.
```

Interlude   E |Dmaj7 |C♯m |Dmaj7 ||

                  E |

Verse 3   Well, good day, sunlight.

        Dmaj7 |

            I'd like to say how truly bright you are.

        C♯m

            You don't know me,

           |Dmaj7 | ||

But I   know you. See, you're my favorite.

Curbside Prophet

Words and Music by
Jason Mraz, Billy Galewood and Christina Ruffalo

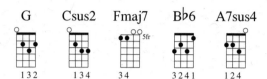

Intro   **G**   **Csus2** |**Fmaj7** **B♭6** **A7sus4** |

            G   **Csus2** |**Fmaj7** **B♭6** **A7sus4**

Chorus 1

       ||**G**   **Csus2**
I'm just a curbside prophet with my hand in my pocket,
   |**Fmaj7**   **B♭6**   **A7sus4**
And I'm waiting for my rocket to come.
    |**G**   **Csus2**
I'm just a curbside prophet with my hand in my pocket,
   |**Fmaj7**   **B♭6** **A7sus4** ||
And I'm waiting for my rocket, y'all.   Hey.

Interlude   **G**   **Csus2** |**Fmaj7** **B♭6** **A7sus4** |

            G   **Csus2** |**Fmaj7** **B♭6** **A7sus4**

Copyright © 2002 Goo Eyed Music (ASCAP), Flozkid Music Publishing (ASCAP),
Original Gangster Of Cleveland (ASCAP), Arufftrip Publishing (ASCAP) and Dopereven Publishing (ASCAP)
All Rights for Flozkid Music Publishing Administered by Original Gangster Of Cleveland
All Rights for Dopereven Publishing Controlled and Administered by Arufftrip Publishing
International Copyright Secured   All Rights Reserved

Verse 1

```
         ‖G                        Csus2
You see, it started way back in NY  -  C
         |Fmaj7                    B♭6    A7sus4
When I stole my first rhyme from the M-I-C
         |G                  Csus2
At-a West End Avenue at      Sixty-three.
         |Fmaj7                B♭6    A7sus4        |G
It's the be - ginning of a leap year, Februar - y,      ninety - six,
                     Csus2
When a guitar, picked it up in the mix.
         |Fmaj7                B♭6        A7sus4
I com - mitted to the licks a like a nickel bag of tricks.
         |G                  Csus2               |
Uh, well,   look at me now. Look at me now.
Fmaj7                    B♭6       A7sus4
Look at me now, now, now,        now.
```

Repeat Chorus 1

Repeat Interlude

Verse 2

```
              ‖G                                        Csus2
Well, then you'll never, da never, da guess what I bet,    bet, bet.
      |Fmaj7                    Bb6              A7sus4              |
And I have      no regrets that I bet      my whole check   -   ing account,
G                        Csus2                      |Fmaj7
   Because it all amounts      to nothing up in the end.
              Bb6      A7sus4              |G
Well, you can only count        that "On the Road Again"
                      Csus2
Will soon be on my radio dial.
              |Fmaj7                  Bb6            A7sus4
And I been paying close attention to the Willie Nelson style.
          |G                        Csus2
Like a,    a band of gypsies on the highway wild,
          |Fmaj7                Bb6        A7sus4  |
As I'm a one man mission on the California skyline.
G                      Csus2
Drive up the coast and I brag and I boast
              |Fmaj7                        Bb6        A7sus4       |
Because I'm picking up my pace. I'm makin' time like Space Ghost.
G                        Csus2                      |
Raising a toast to the high   -  way patrol at the most,
Fmaj7                    Bb6            A7sus4
    But my cruise control's      on coast
              |G                          Csus2
'Cause I'm tour'n' around the nation on ex - tended vacation.
          |Fmaj7                Bb6            A7sus4
See I got Elsa, the dog who exceeds      my limi - tation.
          |G          Csus2
I say,  "I like your style, crazy pound pup.
          |Fmaj7                Bb6              A7sus4
You need a ride? Well, come on, girl. Hop in the truck."
```

Chorus 2

```
      ‖G                    Csus2
With the curbside prophet with my hand in my pocket,
      |Fmaj7                  Bb6   A7sus4
And I'm waiting for my rocket to come.
      |G                    Csus2
I'm just a curbside prophet with my hand in my pocket,
      |Fmaj7                  Bb6   A7sus4
And I'm waiting for my rocket, y'all.
```

Repeat Chorus 2

Verse 3

```
      ‖G                    Csus2
See, I'm a down home brother, red - neck undercover
      |Fmaj7 N.C.
With my guitar here, I'm ready to play.
      |G                    Csus2              |Fmaj7 N.C.
And I'm a sucker for a filly, got a natural ability geared    to freestyle.
      |
Look at my flexibility.
G                        Csus2
Dangerous on the mic, my ghetto hat's cocked right.
      |Fmaj7 N.C.
All the ladies say, "Yo, that kid is crazy."
      |G                    Csus2
We got the backstage Betty's taking more than they can get.
      |Fmaj7 N.C.              Bb6
They say,        "What's up with M-R-A-Z."
```

Outro

```
      A7sus4  ‖G            Csus2
```
Uh, hey, hey, hey, hey. Uh, hey.
```
        |Fmaj7                  B♭6        A7sus4
```
Some - thing's different in my world today.
```
          |G              Csus2    |Fmaj7           B♭6  A7sus4
```
Well, they changed my traffic   signs to a brighter yellow.
```
       |G       Csus2
```
Uh, hey, hey.
```
        |Fmaj7                  B♭6        A7sus4
```
Some - thing's different in my world today.
```
          |G              Csus2    |Fmaj7            B♭6  A7sus4
```
Well, they changed my traffic   signs to a brighter yellow.
```
        |G          Csus2
```
I'm just a curbside proph - et, love,
```
 |Fmaj7          B♭6      A7sus4
```
A curbside brother,   love,
```
 |G                Csus2
```
A curbside brother,   love,
```
 |Fmaj7          B♭6         A7sus4 |G      ‖
```
A curbside … Oh,   come on.

Sleep All Day

Words and Music by
Jason Mraz

Dmaj7   Bm7   Em7   A7sus4   A7   G

Intro

| Dmaj7 | Bm7 | Em7 | A7sus4   A7 |

Scat sing...

| Dmaj7 | Bm7 | Em7 | A7sus4   A7 |

Verse 1

‖ Dmaj7 | Bm7

Well, his after moan though cries, "Oh,   no."

| Em7 | A7sus4   A7

He's building up a shine, but he take it   slow.

| Dmaj7 | Bm7

And he knows it's time to make a change   here,

| Em7 | A7sus4   A7

And time to get away.

| Dmaj7 | Bm7

And he knows it's   time for all the wrong reasons,

| Em7 | A7sus4   A7

Oh, time to end the pain.

Chorus 1

‖ Dmaj7 |

But he   sleep all, we sleep all day,

Bm7 | Em7 | A7sus4   A7

Sleep all, we sleep all day   over.

| Dmaj7 |

Why don't we,   sleep all, we sleep all day?

Bm7 | Em7 | A7sus4   A7

Sleep all, we sleep all day   over.

Copyright © 2002 Goo Eyed Music (ASCAP)
International Copyright Secured   All Rights Reserved

Verse 2

‖**Dmaj7** |
She said, uh,   "What would your mother think of all this?
Bm7
How would your father react?
|**Em7** |**A7sus4**   **A7**
Oh,   would he take it all back, what they've   done?"

                      |
"No way," they said.
Dmaj7 |
Take it, take it." "He said,
Bm7 |**Em7** |
Make it with your own   two   hands."
A7sus4   **A7**
That was my old man, and he said,
|**Em7** |
"If   all is grounded, you should
G |**Dmaj7** |
Go make a mountain out of it,   it."

Verse 3

        ‖**Dmaj7** |**Bm7**
Oh, what a lovely day to have slice of humble pie.
        |**Em7** |**A7sus4**   **A7**
Oh, re - calling of the while we used to drive and drive
             |**Dmaj7** |**Bm7** |**Em7**
Here and there,   going no - where but for us.
               |**A7sus4**   **A7**
Nowhere but the   two of us.
                |**Dmaj7** |**Bm7**
And we knew it was   time to take a chance   here,
    |**Em7** |**A7sus4**   **A7**
And time to compromise our lives just   a little while.
         |**Dmaj7** |**Bm7**
And it was time for all the wrong and lone - ly, lonesome reasons.
    |**Em7** |**A7sus4**   **A7**
But time   is often on my side, but I give it to you tonight.

Chorus 2

‖**Dmaj7** |
And we   sleep all, we sleep all day,

Bm7 |**Em7** |**A7sus4**   **A7**
   Sleep all, we sleep all day   over.

             |**Dmaj7** |
Why don't we,   sleep all, we sleep all day?

Bm7 |**Em7** |**A7sus4 A7**
   We sleep all, we sleep all day o - ver, and over, over and over a - gain.

Verse 4

         ‖**Dmaj7** |
And, as the time   goes by, we get a little bit tired,

Bm7 |**Em7** |**A7sus4**   **A7**
Waking and baked another Marlboro mile   wide.

         |**Dmaj7** |**Bm7**
It's sending the boys   on the run in the time in the hot summer sun

        |**Em7**
To swim beneath, over, out - side.

              |**A7sus4**   **A7**
Still they're reading between the lines.

     |**Dmaj7**
But they re - member the part in the Hallmark card,

    |**Bm7** |
Where they read about the dreams, and they're reaching for the stars

Em7 |**A7sus4**   **A7**
  To hold on a little bit closer to.

       |**Dmaj7** |
Oo, they knew it was time, time to take, a take love,

Bm7 |
  Time to take a chance here,

Em7 |**A7sus4**   **A7**
Time to compromise, to occu - py the lives.

      |**Dmaj7** |**Bm7**
And then there was time for all the wrong rea - sons, oh.

     |**Em7** |**A7sus4**   **A7**   ‖
But, oh, time is often on my side, but I give it to you. Oh, boy.

23

Chorus 3

```
        Dmaj7                          |
            Sleep all, we sleep all day,
Bm7                         |Em7
   Sleep all, we sleep all day    over.
           |A7sus4          A7
La - din  -    din - din - da, okay.
                      |Dmaj7                    |
So, why don't we,       sleep all, we sleep all day?
Bm7                          |Em7          |A7sus4    A7
   Sleep all, we sleep all day    over      and over.
```

Verse 5

```
             ||Dmaj7                              |
She said, "What would your mother think of all this?
Bm7                                  |
   How would your father react? Oh, Lord.
Em7                          |A7sus4          A7
   Would he take it all back, what they've done?"
                  |Dmaj7                      |
"No way," they said. "Take it, take it, take it," he said.
Bm7                          |Em7
"Make it, don't break it with your own   two hands."
        |A7sus4      A7
Said that      was my old man, and he said,
        |Em7                          |G                    ||Dmaj7
"If all,    all is grounded, you should   go make a mountain out of it.
```

Outro

                       |Bm7 |Em7

Lord, go make a mountain out of it, go   on and on and on   and on.

               |A7sus4   A7 |Dmaj7 |Bm7

Well, you should go   on, make a mountain out of   it.

        |Em7 |A7sus4   A7

Hey, love. Go on, go   on and go on

     |Dmaj7 |

And go on and make a mountain.

Bm7 |Em7

   Go on and make a mountain, go   on.

              |A7sus4   A7 |Dmaj7 | ||

You should go   on and make a mountain out of it.

Too Much Food

Words and Music by
Jason Mraz

F#   E   A   C#sus4   C#   Dmaj7   D   C#7   B

Intro   F#   E   A | C#sus4 C# F# | E   A | C#sus4 C# F# |

F#   E   A | C#sus4 C# F# | E   Dmaj7 |

Verse 1

‖ F#   E |
Well, you can say that I'm one curly fry in the box of the regular,

A |
Messing with the flavor, oh, the flavor that you savor.

D   C#7 | F#
Saving me for last, but you better not eat me at all.

| D   C#7 | F#
Living in a fast food bag making friends with the ketchup and salt.

| F#   E
Oh, people say that I'm crazy for not moving on to better things.

| A
Instead I'm sitting 'round trash-talking with the onion rings.

| D   C#7 | F#
But it's much too soon to leave   this easy life.

| D   C#7   · | F#
Pass   me the spoon. Pass   the analytical knife.

Copyright © 2002 Goo Eyed Music (ASCAP)
International Copyright Secured   All Rights Reserved

Chorus 1

                ‖**F♯**
'Cause you're about to get   cut up and get cut down.

    |**A** |**B**
It's all about the wordplay, all about the sound in the tone   of my voice.

                              |**F♯**
You gotta let me make my choice   alone before my food gets cold.

      |**F♯**
Better   shut up or get shot down.

    |**A** |
It's all about the know-how, all just a matter of taste.

B |**F♯**   ‖
    Stop telling me the way I gotta play now.   Too much food on my plate.

Interlude 1   **F♯**   **E**   **A** | **C♯sus4 C♯ F♯**| **E Dmaj7**|

Verse 2

                              ‖**F♯**   **E**
Well, believe it or not,   I supersized my sights   on the surprise

         |**A**
In the cereal box. My stomach's smaller than my eyes.

    |**D**   **C♯7** |**F♯**
So I went to see the doctor and he said turn my head and then cough.

                         |**D**   **C♯7** |**F♯**
I didn't listen to what   he said. Instead,   I couldn't wait to get off.

                      |**F♯**   **E**
He said I can have this but I can't have that.

                    |**A**
I should keep wishing I was living the life of a cat

     |**D**   **C♯7** |**F♯**
But   I ain't the one whose gon - na be missing the feast,

                 |**D**   **C♯7** |**F♯**
Just like you   ain't the one who seems   to be calming the beast.

Chorus 2

‖F♯

Now you're about to get   cut up and get cut down.

|A |B

It's all about the wordplay, all about the sound in the tone   of my voice.

|F♯

You gotta let me make my choice   alone before my food gets cold.

|F♯

You better   shut up or get shot down.

|A |

It's all about the know-how, all just a matter of taste.

B |

  Stop telling me the way that I gotta play.

F♯   ‖

You're putting too much food on my plate. Come on.

Interlude 2   F♯   E   A | C♯sus4 C♯ F♯| E   A |

A   C♯sus4 C♯ F♯| E   A |

Oh, now.

A   C♯sus4 C♯ F♯| E Dmaj7|

Said, "Yeah."

Bridge

‖C♯7 |

Well, if you are what you eat, in my case   I'll be sweet,

|D |A |C♯7

So come   and   get   some.

|C♯7 |D |E

I'm so o-o - ver it.

Chorus 3

‖ F♯
’Cause you’re about to get   cut up and get cut down.
| A |
It’s all about the know-how, all just a matter of taste.
B |
  Stop telling me the way that I gotta play.
F♯ ‖
  You put too much food on my plate. Come on.

Outro

F♯ |
Get up to get, get it and get down.
A |
Get up to get, get it and get down.
B |
Get up to get, get it and up. Well, come on.
F♯ |
Get up, get up, get up. Well, come on.
F♯ |
Get up to get, get it and get some.
A |
Get up to get, get it and get some.
B |
Get up to get, get it and get some.
F♯ | E A|
There’s too much food on my plate. Come on.
A   C♯sus4   C♯ F♯ | E   A|
Yeah, yeah, yeah, yeah, yeah.
A   C♯sus4   C♯ F♯ | E   A|
Well, come on, come on,   come on,   come on.
A   C♯sus4 C♯ F♯| E Dmaj7| ‖
  Ya - da - da - da.

29

Absolutely Zero

Words and Music by
Jason Mraz

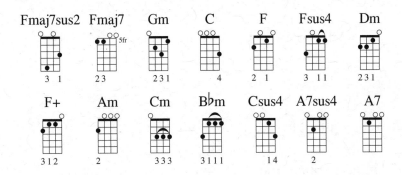

Intro   Fmaj7sus2 |Fmaj7 |Fmaj7sus2 |Fmaj7   ‖

Verse 1

Fmaj7sus2 |Fmaj7 |
You,   you were a friend.

Fmaj7sus2 |Fmaj7
You were a friend of mine. I let you spend   the night.

                                     |Gm |C
You see, how it was my fault.

                         |Fmaj7sus2 |Fmaj7 |
Of course, it was mine.

Fmaj7sus2 |Fmaj7
I'm   too hard at work.

           |Fmaj7sus2 |Fmaj7
Have you ever heard of anything so ab - surd

                         |Gm |C
Ever in your life?

                                     |F   Fsus4 |F   ‖
I'm sorry for wasting your time.

Copyright © 2002 Goo Eyed Music (ASCAP)
International Copyright Secured   All Rights Reserved

Chorus 1

```
            Dm                                  |F+
Who am I to say this situa  -  tion isn't great
                            |Am
When it's my job    to make the most of it?
   |Cm                                    |Gm
Of course, I didn't know that it would hap - pen to me.
   |Bbm            |Fmaj7sus2   |Fmaj7        ||
Not     that easy.
```

Verse 2

```
Fma7sus2                        |Fmaj7
Hey,    what's that you say?
        |Fmaj7sus2                            |Fmaj7
You're not blaming me for anything. Well, that's great,
                        |Gm
But I don't break that eas - y.
   |C             |Fmaj7sus2 |Fmaj7
Does  it fade away?
              |Fmaj7sus2         |Fmaj7
So that's why I'm,       I'm apologiz  -  ing now
   |Fmaj7sus2                            |Fmaj7
For telling you I thought that we could make      it.
                    |Gm
I just don't get enough
       |C                    |F      Fsus4      |F
To believe  that we've both changed.
```

Chorus 2

```
      ‖Dm                              |F+
So who am I to say this situa  -  tion isn't great?
              |Am
It's my time    to make the most of it.
 |Cm                                      |Gm
Of course, I didn't know that it would hap  -  pen to me.
   |B♭m              |F          |Csus4    C
Not     that easy, no,   no, no, no.
 |Dm                                      |F+
If all along the fault is up for grabs,      why can't you have it?
              |Am
If it's for sale,    what is your offer?
    |Cm                                   |Gm
I will sell it for no less than what I bought    it for.
   |B♭m              |F          |Csus4  C    |F          |A7sus4  A7
Pay     no more than ab - solutely ze  -  ro.
```

Bridge

```
         ‖Gm                            |C
Well, neither one of us deserves the blame
            |F       F+              |Dm
Because op - portunities    moved us away.
   |Gm                         |C
It's not an easy thing to learn to play
     |F              F+                |Dm
A game   that's made for two,    that's you and me.
                          |B♭m
The rules remain a mystery.
               |A7sus4  A7
See how it's eas - y.
```

Chorus 3

```
        ‖Dm                            |F+
So, who am I to say this situa  -  tion isn't great?
                        |Am
Well, it's our time    to make the most of it.
         |Cm                                |Gm
How could we ever know that this would hap - pen to me?
       |B♭m              |F              |Csus4   C
Not     that easy, no,   no, ho, ho,
         |Dm                                |F+
When all along the fault is up for grabs,      and there you have it.
                        |Am
Well, it's for sale.    Go make your offer.
         |Cm                                |Gm
Will I sell it for no less than what I bought    it for?
       |B♭m                  |F          |Csus4   C   |F          |
Pay      no more than ab - solutely ze - ro.
         |F        |          ‖
Love,   love.
```

33

On Love, in Sadness

Words and Music by
Jason Mraz and Jenny Keane

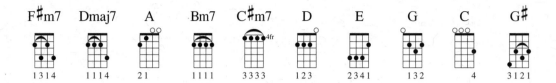

Intro   F#m7 | | | |Dmaj7 | | | |

F#m7 | | | |Dmaj7 | | |

Verse 1

||A | |
Sing about that, oh, love, it's a brittle madness.
Bm7 | |
I sing about it in all my sadness.
C#m7 | |D |
It's not falsified to say that I found God
|A | |
So inevitably well. It still exists,
Bm7 |C#m7
Pale and fine. I can't dismiss and I won't resist.
|C#m7 |D |
And if I die, well, at least I tried.

Copyright © 2002 Goo Eyed Music (ASCAP), Flozkid Music Publishing (ASCAP) and Quiet Span Of Sky Publishing (ASCAP)
All Rights for Flozkid Music Publishing Administered by Quiet Span Of Sky Publishing
International Copyright Secured   All Rights Reserved

Chorus 1

        ‖**A** |**E**
And we just lay awake in lust
   |**Bm7** | |**A**
And rust   in the rain, and pour over everything
                 |**E**
We say we trust.
       |**Bm7** | |**A**
Well, it hap - pened again; I listened in through hall - ways
              |**E**
And thin doors
       |**Bm7** | |**D**
Where the riv - ers unwind, rust and the rain en - dure.
          | | | ‖
The rust and the rain so thin, well, I'm in like Flynn again,

Interlude

F♯m7 | | |
      Yeah.   Hey,
|**Dmaj7** | | |
I will.

Verse 2

    ‖**A** |**Bm7**
So go on and place your order now
   |**C♯m7** |**D** |**A**
'Cause some other time is right around the clock.
   |**Bm7** |**C♯m7** |**D** |**A**
You can stand in line. Well, it fi - n'lly begins, oh, just around the block.
   |**Bm7** |**C♯m7** |**D** |**A**
You can have your pick if your stomach is sick, whether you eat or not.
          |**Bm7** |**A**
And there is just one   thing that I almost forgot.
        |**A**
Oh, see, you and me,

Chorus 2

|| A | E

We just lay awake in lust

| Bm7 | | A

And rust   in the rain, and pour over everything

          | E

We say we trust.

| Bm7 | | A

Well, it hap - pened again; I listened in through hall - ways

         | E

And thin doors

| Bm7 | | A

Where the riv - ers unwind, the rivers unwind so eas - y.

| E | A |

Oh,   these are the comforts that be.

Bridge

|| G | D | C | G

You see, well, I'm feeling luck - y. Oh, well,   maybe that's just me.

| G | D | C | G

Well, you'd be so proud of me. Oh, well,   if you could only see

| G | D | C |

How we're gonna grow on up to be. Ah, yes, we   are thick as thieves.

N.C. G   G♯ | A | Bm7 | C♯m7 | D | A | Bm7 | A |

Scat sing...

Repeat Verse 1

36

Chorus 3

```
              ‖A                 |E
```
And we just lay awake in lust
```
       |Bm7              |                |A
```
And rust   in the rain, and pour over everything
```
                        |E
```
We say we trust.
```
              |Bm7              |                |A
```
Well, it hap - pened again; I listened in through hall - ways
```
                        |E
```
And thin doors
```
              |Bm7              |              |D
```
Where the riv - ers unwind, rust and the rain en - dure.
```
       |D              |         |
```
The rust and the rain endure.   I'm sure because
```
     |A              |E
```
I'm in so far to know
```
              |Bm7              |
```
The measure of love   ain't loss. Love will never ever be
```
   |A              |E
```
In so far to know
```
              |Bm7              |
```
The measure of love   ain't loss. Love will never ever be
```
    |A              |E
```
In so far to know
```
              |Bm7              |              |D        |
```
The measure of love   ain't loss. Love will never ever be lost   on me.
```
       |D              |              ‖
```
Oh, not   tonight. See, love   will never ever be lost

       F♯m7 | | | |Dmaj7 |
```
*Outro*
```
   On me. Love   will   never ever be lost   on me.
   Dmaj7 | |
```
Love will not  be,
```
   Dmaj7 |F♯m7 |
```
Love will never be lost      on me.
```
   F♯m7 | | |Dmaj7 | | | ‖
```
Love    will    not    be     lost   on  me.

37
```

No Stopping Us

Words and Music by
Jason Mraz

Abmaj7   Dbmaj7   Cm7   Bm7   Bbm7   Dbm7   Cbmaj7   Cmaj7   Eb7

1333   1114   3333   2222   1111   3333   4321   2   1113

Intro

|Abmaj7   Dbmaj7 | |Abmaj7   Dbmaj7 | |

|Abmaj7   Dbmaj7 | |Abmaj7   Dbmaj7 |

Verse 1

||Abmaj7   Dbmaj7 |
Would it take a baker's dozen to get my point   to you?
|Abmaj7   Dbmaj7 |
Would it take a half a pound to roll a   joint for you?
|Abmaj7   Dbmaj7 |
Would it take some hailing Mary's so full of grace   to get my sound to you?
|Abmaj7   Dbmaj7 |
Will you help me break it down and get on   through,

Chorus 1

||Cm7 Bm7 |Bbm7 |
Down to the other si - i - i - i - ide.
|Cm7   Bm7 |Bbm7 |
It's easy if you only try, try, try, try.
|Cm7   Bm7 |Bbm7 |
Oh well, don't lie down on the job,   oh, no.
|Dbm7 | |Abmaj7   Dbmaj7 |
Because once we hit the top there's no   stopping us   now.
Dbmaj7 |Abmaj7   Dbmaj7 |
      Ain't no stopping us.

Copyright © 2002 Goo Eyed Music (ASCAP)
International Copyright Secured   All Rights Reserved

Verse 2

      ‖A♭maj7   D♭maj7|
Should I address all my letters to the well   to be?

        |A♭maj7   D♭maj7|
Should I say return to sender's just a   well be done?

       |A♭maj7
Should I better not take it so personally

D♭maj7 |
If   all   the good loving is never received?

      |A♭maj7   D♭maj7|
Baby, if it was me, well, I wouldn't think twice.

Chorus 2

      ‖Cm7 Bm7 |B♭m7
No, not I, I,   I,   I,   I.

   |Cm7   Bm7 |B♭m7
It's easy if you only try, try, try.

     |Cm7   Bm7 |B♭m7
Oh, well, don't lie down on the job   or worse.

    |D♭m7 | |A♭maj7   D♭maj7|
Because once we hit the top there's no stopping us   now.

D♭maj7 |A♭maj7   D♭maj7|
    There's no stopping us.

D♭maj7 |A♭maj7   D♭maj7|
    There's no stopping us   now.

D♭maj7 |A♭maj7   D♭maj7|
    No stopping us.

Bridge

```
  ‖Cbmaj7            |                      |Dbmaj7
```
Oo, I will drive a thousand miles, or I'll meet you at the station.
```
  |Dbmaj7           Cmaj7|Cbmaj7            |
```
If only you would take a va-cation from this thing you have created,
```
  |Dbmaj7                    |Eb7         ‖
```
I promise to make it worth your while.

Interlude

```
    Abmaj7    Dbmaj7|                  |Abmaj7    Dbmaj7|          |
```
                    You know, you know that I'll try.
```
  Abmaj7    Dbmaj7|            |Abmaj7    Dbmaj7|
```


Outro

```
        ‖Cm7   Bm7
```
So, come on, try,   try.
```
        |Bbm7
```
Baby, baby, won't you try.
```
      |Cm7    Bm7           |Bbm7
```
It's easy if you do not run.
```
      |Cm7         Bm7              |Bbm7
```
Well, I promise you you'll have your fun, fun.
```
      |Dbm7                |              |Abmaj7
```
Because once we hit the top we've just begun.
```
    |Dbmaj7                |Abmaj7    Dbmaj7|
```
Oo,   there's no stopping us.
```
Dbmaj7                   |Abmaj7    Dbmaj7|
```
    There's no stopping us,   yeah.
```
Dbmaj7                   |Abmaj7    Dbmaj7|      ‖
```
    There's no stopping us.

The Boy's Gone

Words and Music by
Jason Mraz

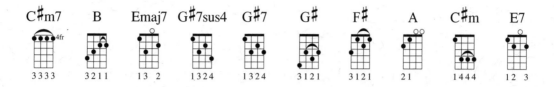

Intro   C♯m7 |B |Emaj7 |G♯7sus4 G♯7 |

C♯m7 |B |Emaj7 |G♯7sus4

G♯7   ‖C♯m7 |B
The boy's   gone.

|Emaj7 |G♯7sus4
The boy's gone   home.

G♯7 |C♯m7 |B
The boy's   gone.

|Emaj7 | | ‖
The boy's gone   home.

Copyright © 2002 Goo Eyed Music (ASCAP)
International Copyright Secured   All Rights Reserved

Verse 1

```
C#m7                  |B                              |Emaj7
      What will hap - pen to a face in the crowd
                    |G#7sus4   G#7 |
When it finally gets too crowded?
C#m7                  |B                              |Emaj7
   And what will hap - pen to the origins of sounds
                    |G#7sus4       |G#7
After all the sounds have sounded?
          |C#m7                              |G#
Well, I hope      I never have to see that day,
          |B                              |F#
But, by God, I know it's headed our way.
          |A              |G#7sus4
So I better be happy now
       G#7     |C#m7            |B
That the boy's go - ing home.
                |Emaj7          |G#7sus4  |G#7   ||
The boy's gone        home.
```

Verse 2

```
C#m7                        |B
      And what becomes    of a day
       |Emaj7                |G#7sus4   G#7 |
For those      who rage against        it?
C#m7                  |B                  |Emaj7
   And who will sum    up the phrase for all      left
                |G#7sus4       |G#7
Standing 'round in        it?
          |C#m7                              |G#
Well, I suppose     we'll all make our judgment calls.
          |B                              |F#
We'll walk it alone,  stand up tall, then march  to the fall.
          |A                    |G#7sus4
And we better be    happy now
       G#7 |C#m7            |B
That we'll all go    home.
                |Emaj7          |G#7sus4  G#7
Yeah, we'll all go      home.
```

Bridge 1

```
       ‖C♯m                      |G♯
Be so happy with the way you are.
          |B                        |F♯
Just be hap - py that you made it this far.
          |A               |
Go on, be    happy now.
          |G♯7sus4          |G♯7
Please, be happy now.
```

Bridge 2

```
                 ‖C♯m              |E7          |A          |G♯7sus4
Because you say that this, this is some - thing else,        alright,
G♯7     |C♯m       |E7              |A              |G♯7sus4
I say that this, this is    something else.      Well, all right.
G♯7         |C♯m           |E7              |A              |G♯7sus4
You say that this, oh,   this   is something, this  is something else.
     G♯7          |C♯m                      |E7
Oo,  thi - di - di this    is, oh, thi - di - di this    is, yeah,
                   |A                    |G♯7sus4 |G♯7
Di - di - di - di this   is, oh, something else.
```

Bridge 3

```
        ‖C♯m                           |G♯
Well, I tried    to live my life and lived it so well.
              |B                          |F♯
But when it's all o - ver is it heaven or is it hell?
             |A                |G♯7sus4
See, I better be happy now
     G♯7        |C♯m7        |B
That no one can      tell.
             |Emaj7  |G♯7sus4
Say, nobody knows.
```

Outro

```
   G#7              ‖C#m                                 |G#
I'm gonna be hap - py with the way that I am.
                     |B                        |F#
I'm gonna be hap - py with all that I stand    for.
                    |A            |G#7sus4
And I'm gonna be  happy now
         G#7     |C#m7        |B
'Cause the boy's go - ing home.
                  |Emaj7        |G#7sus4
The boy's gone       home.
G#7              |C#m7        |B          |Emaj7
Yeah, the boy's
         |G#7sus4
Going home.
G#7              |C#m7        |B          |Emaj7
Yeah, the boy's
         |G#7sus4
Going home.
G#7              |C#m7        |B          |Emaj7
Yeah, the boy's
         |G#7sus4  G#7 |C#m    ‖
Going home.
```

Tonight, Not Again

Words and Music by
Jason Mraz and Jenny Keane

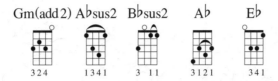

Intro   Gm(add2)|Absus2 |Gm(add2)|Absus2 |Gm(add2)|Absus2 |Gm(add2)|Absus2

Verse 1

||Gm(add2) |Absus2
The night,   she brushed her hand upon my   flushed cheek;

Gm(add2) |Absus2
Smelled of childhood, remnants of a dust - y weeping willow.

Gm(add2) |Absus2
Clouds soothe, they're shredded by the calico;

|Gm(add2) |Absus2
Were oh so vast and quick as I was on   my own now.

Gm(add2)|Absus2 |Gm(add2)|Absus2 ||

Verse 2

Gm(add2) |Absus2
And this time, like every other time,   I believe that I never find

Gm(add2) |Absus2
Another sweet little girl with sequined sea   foam eyes,

Gm(add2) |Absus2 |Gm(add2)
Ocean-lapping voice, smile coy as the brightest quiet span of   sky.

|Absus2
And I'm all alone again   tonight.

|Gm(add2) |Absus2
Not again, not again, not again.

|Gm(add2) |Absus2
Not again, not again, not   again. Mm.

Copyright © 2002 Goo Eyed Music (ASCAP), Flozkid Music Publishing (ASCAP) and Quiet Span of Sky Publishing (ASCAP)
All Rights for Flozkid Music Publishing Administered by Quiet Span of Sky Publishing
International Copyright Secured   All Rights Reserved

Chorus 1

```
        ‖B♭sus2      |                                      |A♭
Mm,           oo.                And don't it feel al - right?
                          |E♭
And don't it feel so  nice?
        |B♭sus2        |A♭          |E♭                      |Gm(add2)
Love  -  ly,  love  -  ly,   love  -  ly. Say, say it again.
        |A♭sus2                  |Gm(add2)  |A♭sus2
Ah,        lovely. Say it again.          Ah.
```

Verse 3

```
        ‖Gm(add2)        |A♭sus2
Well, I'm           unable to inhale all the riches
        |Gm(add2)                        |A♭sus2
As I'm           awkward as a wound on my bones.
            |Gm(add2)                |A♭sus2
Still, I've got        cobblestone joints and plate glass points,
        |Gm(add2)                |A♭sus2
As I'm all by myself tonight. Not a - gain, not again.
```

Chorus 2

```
        ‖B♭sus2      |                                      |A♭
Oo,           oo.                And don't it feel al - right?
                          |E♭
And don't it feel so  nice?
        |B♭sus2        |A♭          |E♭
Love  -  ly,  love  -  ly,   love  -  ly.
        |B♭sus2            |
Say-ay  -  ay  -  ay - ay.
```

Bridge

```
        ‖Ab                                    |Eb
```
And if you should   nervously break down when its   time for the shakedown,
```
        |Bbsus2
```
Would you   take it?
```
                |Ab                      |Eb
```
It's when you   cry just a little but you   laugh in the middle
```
                |Bbsus2
```
That you've   made it.
```
                        |Ab                      |Eb
```
And don't it feel al - right? And don't it feel so   nice?
```
        |Bbsus2              |                    |Ab        |Eb        |
```
Love,   love, love, love.   *Scat sing...*
```
Bbsus2    |          |Ab      |Eb
```

Interlude

```
                              ‖Gm(add2)   |Absus2      |Gm(add2)
```
Say it, say it, say it again.   Love,   love.
```
        |Absus2       |Gm(add2) |Absus2      |Gm(add2)              |Absus2
```
Love.   Love,   so lovely,   lovely to do it again.
```
        |Gm(add2) |Absus2          |Gm(add2) |Absus2
```
It's so love   -   ly to do it again.
```
        |Gm(add2)              |Absus2
```
Again,   oh, loving again.
```
          |Gm(add2)                    |Absus2      |Bbsus2    |        |
```
It's coming again.   It's coming again.
```
Ab    |Eb    |Bbsus2|        |Ab    |Eb    |Bbsus2|Ab    |Eb
```
Scat sing...

Outro

                ‖**Gm(add2)** |**A♭sus2**

Say it, say it, say it again.   Oh,

  |**Gm(add2)** |**A♭sus2** |**Gm(add2)**

So   beautiful.   Tonight,

            |**A♭sus2** |**Gm(add2)** |**A♭sus2** |

It's coming again.   Love,   lovely.

Gm(add2) |**A♭sus2** |**Gm(add2)** |**A♭sus2** |

Love, love. *Scat sing...*

Gm(add2) |**A♭sus2** |**Gm(add2)** |**A♭sus2**   ‖

                  Lovely.

Life Is Wonderful

Words and Music by
Jason Mraz

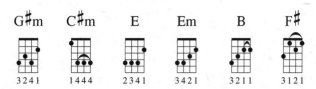

Verse 1

‖G#m |
It takes a crane to build   a crane.
                                        |C#m |
It takes two floors to make a   story.
                                   |E
It takes an egg to make a hen.
                                   |Em
It takes a hen to make an egg.
                                   |B |F#
There is no end to what I'm   saying.

Verse 2

‖G#m |
It takes a thought to make   a word.
                                        |C#m |
And it takes some words to make an   action.
                                  |E
And it takes some work to make it work.
                                  |Em
It takes some good to make it hurt.
                             |B |F#   ‖
It takes some bad for satis - faction.

Copyright © 2005 Goo Eyed Music (ASCAP)
International Copyright Secured   All Rights Reserved

Chorus 1

```
        G#m                        |C#m                    |
Ah, la, la, la, la, la, la. Life    is wonderful.
F#                           |B                    |
Ah, la, la, la, la, la, la. Life    goes full circle.
G#m                         |C#m                    |
   Ah, la, la, la, la. Life    is wonderful.
F#                      |            |G#m    |        |        |
Ah, la, la, la, la.            Mm.
```

Verse 3

```
                              ‖G#m             |
It takes a night to make it    dawn.
                              |C#m                |
And it takes a day to make you yawn, brother.
                              |E
And it takes some old to make you young.
                              |E
It takes some cold to know the sun.
                       |B                    |F#
It takes the one to have    the other.
```

Verse 4

```
                              ‖G#m             |
And it takes no time to fall in love.
                       |C#m                    |
But it takes you years to know what love is.
                              |E
And it takes some fears to make you trust.
                              |E
It takes those tears to make it rust.
                          |B              |F#        ‖
It takes the dust to have it pol - ished.   Yeah.
```

50

Chorus 2

```
G#m                        |C#m              |
Ah, la, la, la, la, la. Life    is wonderful.
  F#                          |B               |
    Ah, la, la, la, la, la. Life    goes full circle.
  G#m                        |C#m              |
    Ah, la, la, la, la, la. Life    is wonderful.
  F#                    |            |G#m        |        |        |
    Ah, la, la, la.          It is,    it is so ...
              |G#m        |        |        |
And it is   so ...
```

Verse 5

```
                              ||G#m              |
It takes some silence to make sound.
                              |C#m              |
And it takes a loss before you found it.
                              |E
And it takes a road to go no - where.
                              |Em
It takes a toll to make you care.
                    |B              |F#             ||
It takes a hole to make a mountain.
```

Chorus 3

```
G#m                        |C#m              |
Ah, la, la, la, la, la. Life    is wonderful.
  F#                          |B               |
    Ah, la, la, la, la, la. Life    goes full circle.
  G#m                      |C#m              |
    Ah, la, la, la, la, la. Life    is wonderful.
  F#                          |B               |
    Ah, la, la, la, la, la. Life    is meaningful.
  G#m                        |C#m              |
    Ah, la, la, la, la, la, la, la. Life  is wonderful.
  F#                    |
    Ah, la, la, la, la, la.
```

Outro

```
     ‖G♯m          |              |              |
     It is    so          wonder - ful.
              |G♯m                   |
     And it is     so  meaning - ful.
          |G♯m               |
     It is    so  wonder - ful.
          |G♯m          |              |              ‖
     It is    meaning - ful.
```

Wordplay

Words and Music by
Jason Mraz and Kevin Kadish

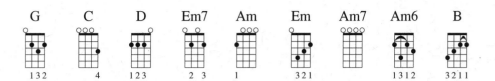

Intro G C |D |G C |D

Verse 1

        ||**Em7**   **G**
I've been all   around the world. I've been a new sensation.
      |**Am**
But it doesn't really matter in this g-generation.
     |**Em7**   **G**
The sophomore slump is an uphill battle,
     |**Am**
And someone said that ain't my scene.
            |**Em7**   **G** |
'Cause they need a new song like a new religion, music for the television.
Am
I can't do the long division. Someone do the math
    |**Em7**   **G** |
'Fore the record label puts me on the shelf up in the freezer.
Am
Got to find another way to live the life of leisure.
    |**Em**   **G**
So I drop my top, mix and I mingle.
   |**Am7** ||
Is everybody ready for the single? And it goes:

Copyright © 2005 Goo Eyed Music (ASCAP), WB Music Corp. (ASCAP), Song Tower (ASCAP) and Slowguy Songs (ASCAP)
All Rights for Song Tower and Slowguy Songs Administered by WB Music Corp.
International Copyright Secured   All Rights Reserved

Chorus 1

```
    G    C        |D
La, la, la, la, la.
                                          |
Now, listen closely to the verse I lay.
G         C        |D
  La, la, la, la, la.
                              |
It's all about the wordplay.
G         C         |D
  I, la, la, la, love

The wonderful thing it does because,
    |Em7                                    D
Be - cause I am the wizard of oohs and ahs and fa la la's,
          |C                                       |G   C   |D
Yeah, the Mister A to Z. They say I'm all about the wordplay.
```

Verse 2

```
                          ‖Em7
When it's time to get ill,
                          G
I got your remedy for those who don't remember me.
      |Am
Well, let me introduce you to my style.
 |Em7                        G
I try to keep a jumble and the lyrics never mumble
          |Am
When the music's making people tongue-tied.
        |Em7                      G                    |
You want a new song like a new religion, music for the television.
Am
I can't do the long division. Someone do the math
        |Em7                      G            |
'Fore the people write me off like I'm a one-hit wonder.
Am
Gotta find another way to keep from going under.
    |Em          Tacet
Pull out the stops.  Got your attention.
  |Am7                                            ‖
I guess it's time again for me to mention the wordplay.
```

```
                    G       C       |D
Chorus 1            La, la, la, la, la.

                                                    |
                    Now, listen closely to the verse I lay.
                    G       C       |D
                      La, la, la, la, la.

                                            |
                    It's all about the wordplay.
                    G       C        |D
                      I, la, la, la, love

                    The wonderful thing it does because,
                      |Em7                              D
                    Be - cause I am the wizard of oohs and ahs and fa la la's,
                            |C                                      |
                    Yeah, the Mister A to Z. They say I'm all about the wordplay.



                            ||Am6
Bridge              I built a bridge across a stream of consciousness.
                                    |B
                    It always seems to be flowing,

                    But I don't know which way my brain is going.
                      |Em                              D
                    All the ryhming and the timing keeps the melodies inside me,
                      |C
                    Ever climbing till I'm running out of air.
                            |Am6                                      |
                    Are you pre - pared to take a dive into the deep end of my head?
                    B                                    |              ||
                      Are you listening to a single word I've said?
```

```
              G     C        |D
Chorus 2    La, la, la, la, la.

                                          |
            Now, listen closely to the words I say.
            G       C        |D
              La, la, la, la, la.

                                    |
            I'm sticking to the wordplay.
            G       C        |D
              I, la, la, la, love

            The wonderful thing it does because,
              |Em7                               D
            Be - cause I am the wizard of oohs and ahs and fa la la's,
                  |C                                        ‖
            Yeah, the Mister A to Z. They say I'm all about the wordplay.
```

```
              G     C        |D
Chorus 3    La, la, la, la, la.

                                    |
            I'm all about the wordplay
            G       C        |D
              La, la, la, la, la.

                                    |
            Sticking with the wordplay.
            G       C        |D
              I, la, la, la, love,

            I love the wonderful thing it does because,
              |Em7                       D
            Be - cause the oohs and ahs and fa la la's. Fall back in love
                  |C                                    |           ‖
            With the Mister A to Z. They say it's all about the wordplay.
```

Geek in the Pink

Words and Music by
Jason Mraz, Kevin Kadish, Scott Storch and Ian Sheridan

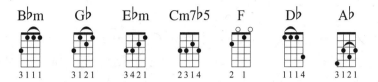

Intro

| B♭m | | G♭ | |
Do, do, do, do, do, do,   do, do, do, do, do.
| E♭m | | Cm7♭5 | F |
Do, do, do, do, do, do,   do, do, do, do, do.

Verse 1

B♭m
  Well, let the geek in the pink take a stab at it.
G♭
  If you like the way I'm thinking, baby, wink at it.
E♭m
  I may be skinny at times, but I'm fat full of rhymes.
D♭   **A♭**
  Pass me the mic and I'm-'ll grab at it.
    |**B♭m**
Well, isn't it delicious crazy way that I'm kissing this.
    |**G♭**
Baby, listen to this. Don't wanna miss it while it's hittin'.
E♭m
  Sometimes you gotta fit in to get in,
  |**D♭**   **F**
But   don't ever quit 'cause soon I'm gonna let you in. Well, see,

Copyright © 2005 Goo Eyed Music (ASCAP), WB Music Corp. (ASCAP), Song Tower (ASCAP), Slowguy Songs Inc. (ASCAP),
Reservoir Media Music (ASCAP), Donkeyfiddle Music (ASCAP) and No BS Publishing (ASCAP)
All Rights for Song Tower and Slowguy Songs Inc. Administered by WB Music Corp.
All Rights for Reservoir Media Music Administered by Reservoir Media Management, Inc.
All Rights for Donkeyfiddle Music Administered by No BS Publishing
International Copyright Secured   All Rights Reserved

Chorus 1

    B♭m   **|G♭**
I don't care what you might think about me.
            |E♭m   **|Cm7♭5**   **F**
You'll get   by without me if you want.
                     |B♭m
Well, I could be the one to take you home.
                   |G♭
Baby, we could rock the night alone.
               |E♭m
If we never get down, it wouldn't be a let-down.
                  |Cm7♭5   **F**
But, sugar, don't for - get what you already know:
                 |B♭m
That I could be the one to turn you out.
              |G♭
We could be the talk across the town.
             |E♭m
Don't judge it by the color, confuse it for another.
          |D♭   **A♭**
You might re - gret what you let slip a - way,
                 |B♭m   **|G♭**   **|**
Like the geek in the pink. Do, do, do, do, do, do, do, do, do, do, do.
E♭m   **|Cm7♭5**   **F**
Do, do, do, do, do, do, do,   do, do, do, do, do.

Verse 2

    ‖**B♭m**
All my re‑lationship fodder don't mean to bother nobody.
    |**G♭** |
But Cupid's automatic must've fired multiple shots at her,
E♭m
 Because she fall in love too often; that's what's the matter.
 |**D♭**   **A♭**
At least when I'm talking about her, keep a patter to flattery.
   |**B♭m**
And she was staring through the doorframe
   |**G♭** |
And eyeing me down like already a bad boyfriend.
E♭m
 Well, she can get her toys out of the drawer, then.
   |**D♭**   **F**   ‖
'Cause I ain't comin' home. I don't need that attention. See,

Chorus 2

B♭m |**G♭**
I don't care what you might think about me.
   |**E♭m** |**Cm7♭5** **F**
She'll get by without me if she wants.
     |**B♭m**
Well, I could be the one to take her home.
    |**G♭**
Baby, we could rock the night alone.
   |**E♭m**
If we never get down. It wouldn't be a let down.
    |**Cm7♭5**   **F**
But, sugar, don't for‑get what you already know:
    |**B♭m**
That I could be the one to turn you out.
   |**G♭**
We could be the talk across the town.
   |**E♭m**
Don't judge it by the color, confuse it for another.
   |**D♭**   **A♭** ‖
You might re‑gret what you let slip a‑way.

Bridge

      G♭   **|B♭m**

             Hey, baby, look at me go

          |F

From zero to hero.

                       |B♭m

You better take it from a geek like me.

      |G♭   **|B♭m**

Well, I can save you from unoriginal dumb - dumbs

                     |Cm7♭5   **|F**

Who wouldn't care if you com   -   plete them or not.

Verse 3

               ‖B♭m

So what? I got a short attention span, a Coke in my hand,

             |G♭

Because I'd rather have the afternoon relaxing.

                 |E♭m   **|**

Understand my hip-hop in flip-flops, well, it don't stop with the light rock.

D♭   **A♭**   **F**   **|**

  My shot to mock you kinda puts me in the tight spot.

B♭m

  The hype is nothing more than hoo-hah,

             |G♭   **|**

So I'm de - veloping a language and I'm calling it my own.

E♭m   **|**

  So, take a peek into the speaker and you'll see what I mean:

D♭   **A♭**   **F**   **‖**

  That on the other side the grass is green - er.

Chorus 3

   B♭m |**G♭**
I don't care what you might think about me.
       |**E♭m** |**Cm7♭5**   **F**
You'll get   by without me if you want.
           |**B♭m**
Well, I could be the one to take you home.
       |**G♭**
Baby, we could rock the night alone.
      |**E♭m**
If we never get down. It wouldn't be a let down.
        |**Cm7♭5**   **F**
But, sugar, don't for - get what you already know:
         |**B♭m**
That I could be the one to turn you out.
      |**G♭**
We could be the talk across the town.
       |**E♭m**
Don't judge it by the color, confuse it for another.
     |**D♭**   **A♭**
You might re - gret what you let slip a - way,
        |**B♭m** |
Like the geek in the pink. Do, do, do, do, do, do,
G♭ |
   Do, do, do, do, do. Well, I'm the geek in the pink.
E♭m |**Cm7♭5**   **F**
Do, do, do, do, do, do, do. Geek is the color for fall.
       |**B♭m** |
I'm the geek in the pink. Do, do, do, do, do, do,
G♭ |
   Do, do, do, do, do. In the pink, yo.
E♭m |**D♭**   **A♭**
Do, do, do, do, do, do, do. Geek is the color for fall.
       |**B♭m** ||
I'm the geek in the pink.

Did You Get My Message?

Words and Music by
Jason Mraz and Dan Wilson

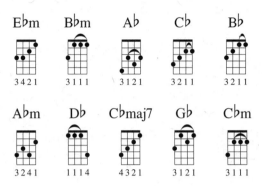

Intro   Ebm   Bbm |Ab   Cb   Bb |Ebm   Bbm |Ab   Cb   Bb |

Ebm   Bbm |Ab   Cb   Bb |Ebm   Bbm |Ab   Cb   Bb

Verse 1

      ||Ebm   Bbm
Did you get my message, the one I left?
          |Ab   Cb
Well, I was trying to condense everything   that I meant
Bb |Ebm   Bbm
In a minute or less when I called   to confess
           |Ab   Cb
And make all   of my stresses go bye - bye.
Bb |Ebm   Bbm
Did you get my message? You didn't, I guess,
         |Ab   Cb
'Cause if you did, you would've called me with your   sweet intent.
Bb |Ebm   Bbm
And we could give it a rest instead of beating our breast
       |Ab   Cb   Bb ||
And making all of the pressure go sky   high.

Copyright © 2005 Goo Eyed Music (ASCAP), Chrysalis Music (ASCAP) and Sugar Lake Music (ASCAP)
All Rights for Chrysalis Music and Sugar Lake Music Administered by BMG Rights Management (US) LLC
International Copyright Secured   All Rights Reserved

Pre-Chorus 1

```
               Abm                                        |Db              Bb
        Do you ever wonder what happens to the words that we send?
                    |Ebm                    Db
Do they bend,    do they break from the flight   that they take
    |Ab                                                  |Abm
And come back together again with a whole new mean - ing
                                        |Db           Bb
And a brand-new sense, com - pletely unrelated to the one I sent?
```

Chorus

```
             ||Cb             Cbmaj7  |Abm        Db
Did you get my message?      Ooh, ooh, ooh.
                    |Ebm              Db        |Ab
Oh, did you get my message?
                    |Cb                 Cbmaj7  |Abm     Db        ||
Oh, did you get my message? Yeah, ooh, ooh, ooh,     hoo.
```

Verse 2

```
        Ebm        Bbm
        Uh oh! Where did it go?
            |Ab                             Cb          Bb     |
Must've bypassed your phone and flown right out of the win - dow.
Ebm        Bbm
        Oh well, how can I tell?
              |Ab                       Cb          Bb
Should I call the operator? Oh, maybe she knows the in - fo
    |Ebm                    Bbm
Or whether or not if my message you got
            |Ab                Cb
Was too much or a lot to re - ply.
        Bb   |Ebm                              Bbm
Why  not try this for a fact (well, should you ever call back)?
            |Ab                        Cb          Bb ||
I'd re - lax and be relieved of all my panic attacks.
```

Pre-Chorus 2

G♭ |C♭   C♭m |
Ah, ah, ah, ah, ooh, ooh, ooh, ooh.
G♭ |C♭   C♭m
Ah, ah, ah, ah, ooh, ooh.

Repeat Chorus

Interlude

E♭m   B♭m |A♭   C♭
         So, d-d-d-d-do   you now?
      B♭ |E♭m   B♭m |A♭   C♭
Arr, d-do do do   d-do.   Arr, d-do do ooh.

Verse 3

B♭   ‖E♭m   B♭m
Oh, did you get my message, the one I left?
        |A♭   C♭
Well, I was trying to condense everything that I meant.
B♭ |E♭m   B♭m
Now the moment has passed. (Not much sand in the glass.)
      |A♭   C♭ B♭‖
And I'm standing to lose my mind.

Pre-Chorus 3

A♭m |D♭   B♭
   Do you ever wonder what happens to the words that we send?
      |E♭m   D♭
Do they bend, do they break from the flight that they take
 |A♭ |A♭m
And come back together again with a whole new mean - ing

To the matter of our love's defense?
 |D♭   B♭
At least be sympathetic to the time I spent.

Repeat Chorus

Outro

        ‖Gb |Cb   Cbm
Did you get my message?

        |Gb |Cb   Cbm
Did you get my message?

        |Gb |
Did you get my message, love,

Cb   Cbm
 That I want to get back with you?

        |Gb
Did you get my message, love,

   |Cb   Cbm
That I want to reconnect with you?

        |Gb
Did you get my message now?

         |Cb   Cbm   ‖
So, why don't you answer the phone?

Mr. Curiosity

Words and Music by
Jason Mraz, Lester Mendez and Dennis Morris

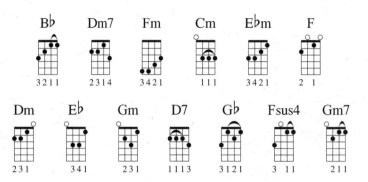

Intro   Bb |Dm7 |Fm |Cm |Ebm |Bb |Cm |F ||

Verse 1

Bb |Dm
Hey, Mister Curiosity,

                              |Fm
Is it true what they've been saying about you?

            |Cm
Are you killing me?

            |Ebm
You took care of the cat already.

            |Bb |Cm
And for those who think it's heavy, is it the truth

            |F ||
Or is it only gos - sip?

Copyright © 2005 Goo Eyed Music (ASCAP), EMI Blackwood Music Inc. (BMI), Apollinaire Music (BMI),
Dirtysick Publishing (ASCAP) and Flozkid Music Publishing (ASCAP)
All Rights for Apollinaire Music Controlled and Administered by EMI Blackwood Music Inc.
All Rights for Dirtysick Publishing Administered by Flozkid Music Publishing
International Copyright Secured   All Rights Reserved

Verse 2

B♭ |Dm
Call it mystery or anything,
           |Fm
Just as long as you'd call me.
        |Cm
I sent the message on. Did you get it when I left it?
   |E♭m
See, this catastrophic event,
   |B♭
It wasn't meant to mean no harm.
    |Cm |F ||
But to think there's nothing wrong is a prob - lem.

Chorus 1

E♭ |B♭
  I'm looking for love this time,
   |Dm |Gm   F |
Sounding hopeful but it's making me cry.
E♭ |B♭
  Love is a mys - tery.
  |D7 | ||
Mister Curious,   come back to me.

Verse 3

B♭ |Dm
  Mister Waiting, ever pa - tient, can't you see
     |Fm
That I'm the same the way you left me?
   |Cm
In a hurry to spell-check me.
    |E♭m |B♭
And I'm underlined already in envy green and pencil red.
     |Cm
And I've for - gotten what you said.
    |F
Will you stop working for the dead

Verse 4

```
          ‖Bb                                        |Dm
And re -turn, Mister Curious? Well I need      some inspiration.
              |Fm                            |Cm
It's my birthday and I cannot find no cause      for celebration.
              |Ebm                      |Bb
The sce - nario is grave, but I'll be braver when you save me
              |Cm                        |F            ‖
From this situation laden with hear - say.
```

Chorus 2

```
       Eb                       |Bb
     I'm looking for love   this time,
          |Dm                              |Gm      F        |
Sounding hopeful but it's making me cry.
       Eb                   |Bb
     And love is a mys - tery.
          |D7                          |                    ‖
Mister Curiousity, be Mister Please  Do Come And Find Me.
```

Bridge

```
    Gm        |Gb     |Gm      |Gb          |
                     Find,      find me,
    Ebm     |Bb     |Ebm          |F         |Fsus4      ‖
    Find      me,      find me.
```

Interlude

```
    Bb     |Dm     |Fm      |Cm     |Ebm     |Bb     |Cm       |F        ‖
```
Operatic falsetto vocal ad lib...

Chorus 3

E♭ |B♭
  I'm looking for love this time,
  |Dm |Gm
Sounding hopeful but it's making me cry,
   F |E♭ |B♭
Trying not to ask why. This love is a mys - tery.
  |D7 |
Mister Curiousity, be Mister Please Do Come And Find Me.
   |E♭ |B♭
Love is blinding when the timing's never right.
    |D7
Or who am I to beg for difference?
  |Gm   F |E♭
Finding love in just an in - stant, well, I don't mind.
    |B♭ |D7
At least I've tried. Well, I tried,
  |D7 |Gm7 | ||
I tried.

Clockwatching

Words and Music by
Jason Mraz, Dennis Morris and Ainslie Henderson

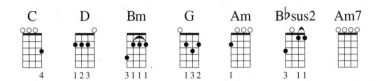

Intro

C |D |Bm |C | |D |Bm |C ||

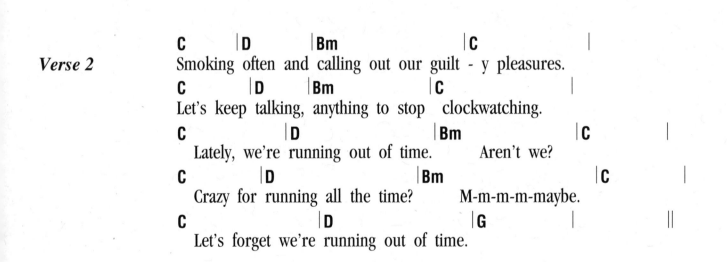

Verse 1

C |D |Bm |C |
Take off both your shoes and clothes; I'll follow.
C |D |Bm |C |
Undo corkscrew. Drink from a half of a bro - ken bottle.
C |D |Bm |C | ||
  Lately, we're running out of time,   aren't we?

Verse 2

C |D |Bm |C |
Smoking often and calling out our guilt - y pleasures.
C |D |Bm |C |
Let's keep talking, anything to stop   clockwatching.
C |D |Bm |C |
  Lately, we're running out of time.   Aren't we?
C |D |Bm |C |
  Crazy for running all the time?   M-m-m-m-maybe.
C |D |G | ||
  Let's forget we're running out of time.

Copyright © 2005 Goo Eyed Music (ASCAP), Dirtysick Publishing (ASCAP), Flozkid Music Publishing (ASCAP) and No BS Publishing (ASCAP)
All Rights for Dirtysick Publishing Administered by Flozkid Music Publishing
International Copyright Secured   All Rights Reserved

Chorus 1

```
    G               D    |       |Am        |          |
    I'm off like an aer  -  oplane.
    G               D    |          |Am       |         |
    I'm licking your post - age stamp again.
    G               D    |     |Am       |         |        |
    I'm using my right   brain and I'm praying that we don't crash.
Bbsus2            Am7  |      |G      |       |
    Who knew I'd come   so fast?
Bbsus2            Am7  |                |G       |        |
    But so what if a two - pump chump can't last.
Bbsus2          C    |
    But I made it to three,
            |G               |
And I fore - closed a five-minute  fantasy
       |Bbsus2              |Am7       |        |
On a short   -   lived flight making love   on economy.
```

Verse 3

```
       ||C         |D    |Bm           |C        |
No jumping con - clusions. I don't think there's no  solution.
    C    |D       |Bm          |C        |
Let's get backwards and for - get our restless des - tination.
    C         |D          |Bm        |C       |
    Let's live in the moment just this time.     Could we
    C       |D        |Bm             |C      |
    Just take one moment of our time?    M-m-m-m-maybe.
    C         |D       |G     |    ||
    Let's forget we're running out of time.
```

Chorus 2

```
         G            D    |        |Am        |          |
      I'm off like an aer  -  oplane.
         G               D    |          |Am       |          |
      I'm catching my sec  -  ond wind again.
         G           D   |       |Am          |          |
      I'm using my left     brain and I'm righting all my wrongs.
      Bbsus2            Am7|      |G      |          |
         I'm yearning to turn   you on.
      Bbsus2                    Am7|                 |G      |          |
         I've been working on get - ting you off, so get on  -  board.
      Bbsus2            C     |
         Well, how can I guess  by the subject
   |G              |
Of   the best predicate that's  left unsaid?
         |Bbsus2            |
When the matter is too delicate,
         |Am7           |         |        |        ||
My lone  -  liness is evident.
```

Interlude 1

```
       C     |D    |Bm    |C    |        |D    |Bm    |C
```

Bridge

```
            ||C
And  its you;
            |D                    |
You're running through my mind,
Bm                         |C          ||
      And it makes me crazy, cra-cra-crazy.
```

72

Interlude 2   C |D |Bm |C | |D |Bm |C |

                           C |D |Bm |C | |D |Bm |C ||

Verse 4

C |D |Bm |C |

Lady dreamer, you might be the sound - est sleeper.

C |D |Bm |C | ||

Tonight, sleep tight and build your nest upon my shoulder.

Bella Luna

Words and Music by
Jason Mraz and William Galewood

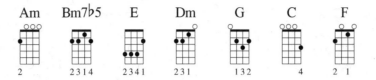

Intro   Am | |Bm7♭5 | | | E |Am | | ‖

Verse 1

Am |
Mystery the moon,
 |**Bm7♭5** |
A hole in the sky,
 |**Bm7♭5**   · |
A supernatural nightlight,
 |**Am** |
So full but often wry.
                 |**Dm** |
A pair of eyes,   a closing one,
         |**Am** |
A chosen child of golden sun.
           |**Bm7♭5** |
A marble dog   that chases cars to farthest reaches of the beach
             |**E** | ‖
And far beyond into the swimming sea of stars.

Interlude 1   Am |Bm7♭5 | E | |Am |Bm7♭5 | E |

Copyright © 2005 Goo Eyed Music (ASCAP), Original Gangsters Of Cleveland (ASCAP) and Flozkid Music Publishing (ASCAP)
All Rights for Original Gangsters Of Cleveland Administered by Flozkid Music Publishing
International Copyright Secured   All Rights Reserved

Verse 2

```
            ‖ Am                        |
The cosmic      fish, they love to kiss.
            | Bm7♭5                     |
They're giving birth to constellations.
            | Bm7♭5          |
No riffs, and, oh, no reser - vation.
            | Am                    |                    |
If they should fall, you get a wish or dedi - cation.
Dm              |                    |
    May I sug - gest you get the best
Am              |                    |
    For nothing less than you and I.
Bm7♭5                          |
        Let's take a chance     as this romance is rising,
    | E                  |              ‖
Oh,    before we lose the lighting.
```

Chorus 1

```
Dm      | G                        | C
        Oh, Bella, Bella, please,
        | F          | Dm              |
Bella, you      beautiful luna.
Dm                          | E        |          ‖
    Oh, Bella, do what you     do.
```

Repeat Interlude 1

Verse 3

|| Am
You are an il - luminating anchor
| Bm7♭5
Of leagues too infinite in number,
| Bm7♭5
Crashing waves and breaking thunder,
| Am
Tiding the ebb and flows of hunger.
Dm
     You're dancing naked there for me.
| Am
You ex - pose all memory. You make the most of boundary.
| Bm7♭5
You're the ghost   of royalty imposing love.
| E
You are the queen and king com - bining everything,
| E
Inter - twining like a ring

Pre-Chorus 1

|| Am | Dm
Around the finger of a girl.
| G | C
I'm just a singer; you're the world.
| F
All I can bring ya
| Dm | E | ||
Is the lan - guage of a lov - er.

Chorus 2

Am | Dm | G
     Bella Lu - na,
| C | F
My beautiful, beautiful moon,
| Dm | E | ||
How you swoon   me like no oth - er,   oh.

Interlude 2   **Am** | |**Bm7♭5** | | |**Am** | |

              Am | |**Bm7♭5** | | |**Am** | ||·

Pre-Chorus 2
```
Dm                            |                      |Am
    May I sug - gest you get the best of your wish.
                              |Am                        |Bm7♭5
May I insist, at no con - test for little you or smaller I,
      |Bm7♭5                       |E
A larger chance at what all there may lie    on the rise,
      |E                     ||
On the brink of our lives.
```

Chorus 3
```
Dm      |G           |C
          Bella,  plea - ee - ee - ease,
          |F        |Dm            |
Bella, you     beautiful luna,
Dm                        |E        |          ||
    Oh, Bella, do what you      do.
```

Repeat Chorus 2

Outro   **Am** |**Bm7♭5** | **E**| |**Am** |**Bm7♭5** | |**E** |**Am** ||

Plane

Words and Music by
Jason Mraz and Dennis Morris

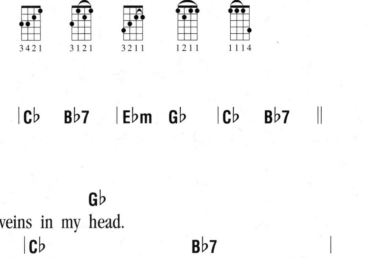

Intro   Ebm Gb |Cb Bb7 |Ebm Gb |Cb Bb7 ||

Verse 1

     Ebm   Gb
Drain the veins in my head.
            |Cb   Bb7
Clean out the reds in my eyes to get by security lines.
     Ebm   Gb
    Dear X-ray ma - chine,
                |Cb   Bb7
Pretend you don't know me so well. I won't tell if you lie.
     Ebm   Gb
Cry 'cause the drought's been brought up.
             |Cb   Bb7
Drinkin' 'cause you're looking so good in your Star - bucks cup.
     |Ebm   Gb
I com - plain for the company that I keep.
             |Cb   Bb7
The window's for sleeping; rearrange. Well, I'm no - body.

Copyright © 2005 Goo Eyed Music (ASCAP), Dirtysick Publishing (ASCAP) and Flozkid Music Publishing (ASCAP)
All Rights for Dirtysick Publishing Administered by Flozkid Music Publishing
International Copyright Secured All Rights Reserved

Chorus 1

            ‖**Cb**
Well, who's laughing now?
            Gb |
I'm leaving your town again.
Bb7 |**Cb**
    And I'm over the ground that you've been spin‑ning.
                      Gb |**Bb7**
And I'm up in the air, so, baby, hell, yeah!
                                     |
Well, honey, I can see your house from here.
Cb   **Gb** |
    If the plane goes down, damn,
Bb7 |
    Well, I'll remember where the love was found.
Cb   **Gb** |**Bb7**   ‖
    If the plane goes down, damn.

Verse 2

    Ebm   **Gb**
Damn! I should be so lucky.
                 |**Cb**
Even only twen‑ty-four hours under your touch,
Bb7
You know I need you so much.
 |**Ebm**   **Gb** |**Cb**
I,   I cannot wait to call you and tell you that I land‑ed
                                Bb7 |
Somewhere and hand you a square   of the airport
Ebm   **Gb** |
    And walk you through the maze of the map that I'm gazing at,
Cb   **Bb7**
Gracefully unnamed and feeling guilty
                                |
For the luck and the look that you gave me.
 Ebm   **Gb**
    You make me somebod‑y.
                 |**Cb**   **Bb7**   ‖
Oh, nobody knows   me. Not even me can see it, yet I bet I'm

Chorus 2

      Cb   Gb |
Leaving your town again.

Bb7 |Cb
And I'm over the ground that you've been spin - ning.

                         Gb |Bb7
And I'm up in the air,   so, baby, hell, yeah!

                                               |
Well, honey, I can see your house from here.

Cb   Gb |
If the plane goes down,   damn,

Bb7 |
I'll remember where the love was found.

Cb   Gb |Bb7 ||
If the plane goes down,   damn.

Interlude   Ebm Db |Cb |Ebm Gb |Cb Bb7

Bridge

                ||Ebm Db |Cb
You get me high - minded.

              |Ebm Gb |Cb Bb7 ||
You keep me high.

Verse 3

Ebm   Gb |Cb
    Flax seeds, well, they tear me o - pen
                      Bb7 |
And supposedly you could crawl right through me.
Ebm   Gb |
    Taste these teeth, please,
Cb   Bb7
And undress me from the sweaters.
                  |Ebm   Gb |
Better hurry, 'cause I'm   heating upward bound now.
Cb   Bb7
    Oh, maybe I'll build my house on your cloud.
      |Ebm   Gb |
Here I'm   tumbling   for you,
Cb   Bb7 ||
Stumbling through the work that I have to do. Don't mean to harm you

Chorus 3

Cb   Gb |
    By leaving your town again.
Bb7 |Cb
    But I'm over the quilt that you've been spin - ning.
                  Gb |Bb7
And I'm up in the air, so, baby, hell, yeah!
                              |Cb
Well, honey, I can see your house from here.
              Gb |
If the plane goes down,   damn,
Bb7 |
    I'll remember where the love was found.
Cb   Gb |
    If the plane goes down,   damn,
Bb7 |
    I'll remember where the love was found.
Cb   Gb |
    If the plane goes down,   damn,
Bb7 |
    I'll remember where the love was found.
Cb   Gb |Bb7 ||
    If the plane goes down, damn,   damn,   damn.

Outro   E♭m G♭ |C♭   B♭7

 |E♭m G♭ |C♭   B♭7
Damn.
 |E♭m G♭ |C♭   B♭7
You get me high.
 |E♭m G♭ |C♭   B♭7
You keep me high - minded.
 |E♭m G♭ |C♭   B♭7
You get me high.
 |E♭m G♭ |C♭   B♭7 |E♭m ||
You get me high - minded.

O, Lover

Words and Music by
Jason Mraz and Dennis Morris

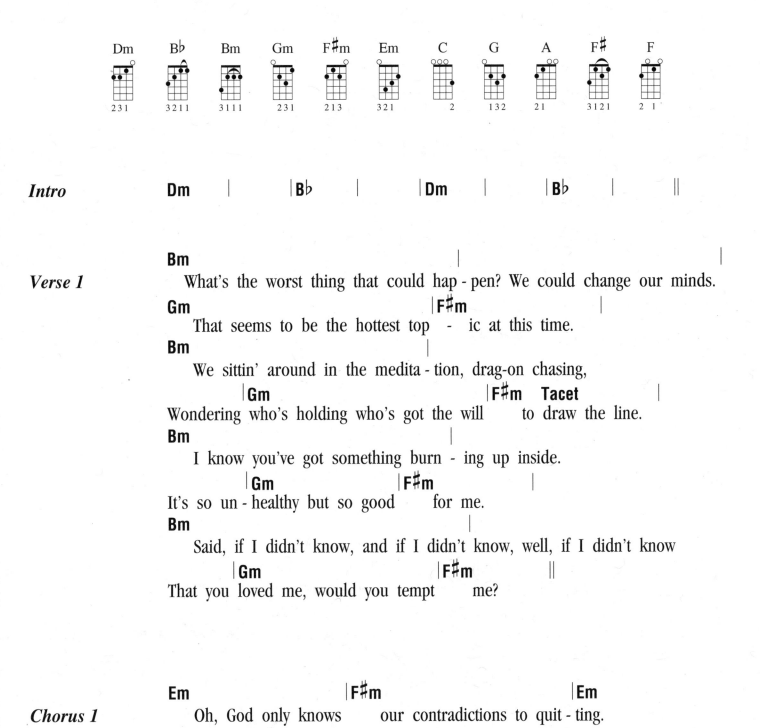

Intro

|: Dm | | Bb | | Dm | | Bb | | :||

Verse 1

Bm
    What's the worst thing that could hap - pen? We could change our minds.
Gm |F#m
    That seems to be the hottest top - ic at this time.
Bm
    We sittin' around in the medita - tion, drag-on chasing,
      |Gm |F#m   **Tacet**
Wondering who's holding who's got the will   to draw the line.
Bm
    I know you've got something burn - ing up inside.
      |Gm |F#m
It's so un - healthy but so good   for me.
Bm
    Said, if I didn't know, and if I didn't know, well, if I didn't know
    |Gm |F#m
That you loved me, would you tempt   me?

Chorus 1

Em |F#m |Em
    Oh, God only knows   our contradictions to quit - ting.
    |F#m |Em
It's a hate - to - love relationship thing.
    |F#m |Em
A fire un - der you is so fulfill - ing.
       |F#m
I feel there's noth - ing more.

Copyright © 2005 Goo Eyed Music (ASCAP), Dirtysick Publishing (ASCAP) and Flozkid Music Publishing (ASCAP)
All Rights for Dirtysick Publishing Administered by Flozkid Music Publishing
International Copyright Secured   All Rights Reserved

Verse 2

‖**Bm** |
I'm giving, giving you the choke hold.

|**Gm** |**F♯m**
My flirting with disaster is mod - ern love.

|**Bm** |
Ooh, you,   you're so bold.

|**Gm** |**F♯m**
My wanting to kiss you still is not enough.

|**Bm** |
I'm getting over   all the comments.

|**Gm** |**F♯m**
Unfriendly statements made by people of non - sense.

|**Bm** |
I'm getting stronger   by the minute.

|**Gm** |**F♯m**
And once I slip into position, I'll swing   you

Chorus 2

‖**Em**
And turn you all a - round.

|**F♯m** |**Em**
You are the sweet - est thing I've found since whenev - er.

|**F♯m** |**Em**
You're the only way my time is measured.

|**F♯m** |**Em**
You might be the silent type, but you're ad - vertising louder now.

|**F♯m** ‖
It's crazy how you're killing me.

Interlude 1

Dm | |**B♭** |
You're killing me.

Verse 3

|| Bm |
But I like your   red top and matching bottoms.

Bm |
You know the ones, the ones you've got on.

Gm | F♯m |
Pull 'em over your skinny self, but don't cover your tattoo. *Whoo!*

Bm | |
'Cause I like to look at you, yeah.   I love that smell on you.

Gm | F♯m |
And I got your special place against   this face for tasting, too.

Bm | |
And I like it natural;   no need for chemicals.

Gm | F♯m |
Sparking it up my senses, you're making the sense.   You call it sexual.

Bm | |
And you're going to get yours, my lady.   Might even be today.

Gm | F♯m ||
And it ain't no thing, 'cause I'll be rolling right along with you.

Chorus 3

Em | F♯m | Em
You are the sweet - est thing I've found since whenev - er.

                     | F♯m | Em
You're the only way my time is measured.

                     | F♯m | Em
You might be the silent type, but you're ad - vertising louder now.

  | F♯m ||
It's crazy how you're killing me.

Bridge

```
        Bm                          |C
            And give us both a break.
                                 |G                      |A
        And give us back a taste    when the way things were
                    F♯              |
        Before they made the laws.
        Bm                          |C
            And give us both a chance.
                                |G
        But it won't be the last    romance,
                          |A              F♯              ||
        'Cause when the weekend starts, the guilty party's on.
```

Interlude 2

```
        Dm            |         |B♭        |         |Dm        |         |

        B♭            |         |F         |         |A         |F♯       ||
```

Outro

```
        Bm                      |                        Gm|
            Weekend party's over.    Don't stop; let's get clos-er.
        Gm                          F♯m|                    Bm  |
            Friday, got cold should-er.    Monday, got a new compo-sure.
        Bm                      |                        Gm|
            Weekend party's over.    Don't stop; let's get low-er.
        Gm                          F♯m|              Bm  |
            I won't blow your cov-er.    Opportunistic lov-er.
        Bm                      |                        Gm|
            Weekend party's over.    Don't stop; let's get clos-er.
        Gm                      F♯m|                        Bm  |
            Friday was medio-cre.    Monday, I'm self-exposed, uh?
        Bm                      |                        Gm|
            Weekend party's over.    Don't stop; let's suppose-a.
        Gm                          F♯m|                    Bm||
            I won't blow your cov-er.    Opportunistic lov-er.
```

Please Don't Tell Her

Words and Music by
Jason Mraz and Eric Hinojosa

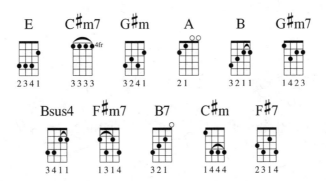

Intro　　　E　　　　|C♯m7　　|G♯m　　|A　　B

Verse 1

　　　　　　　　||E
I hear she's kickin' ass across the board
　　　　　　　　　　　　　　　　|C♯m7
And rocked two hundred thousand, highest score,
　　　　　　　　　　　　　　　　　　　　|G♯m7
And just in time to save the world of being taken over.
　　　　　　　　|A　　Bsus4　B
She's a war - rior.
　　　　　|E
I couldn't play again because the game, it never ended.
　　　|C♯m7
Never even landed on the canon.
　　　　　　　　　　　　|G♯m7
Never let me in to spend my quar - ter.
　　　　　|A　　Bsus4　B　　||
There's no love for me　　no more.

Copyright © 2005 Goo Eyed Music (ASCAP), De Luz Music (ASCAP) and No BS Publishing (ASCAP)
International Copyright Secured   All Rights Reserved

Brtidge 1

F#m7 |B7
Say it isn't so,

            |G#m |C#m
How she easily come,   and she easy go.

     |F#m7 |B7 |
Please don't tell her that I've been meaning to miss her,

            ||
Because I don't.

Interlude 1   E |C#m7 |G#m7 |A   B

Verse 2

              ||E
She was the girl with the broadest shoulders.

          |C#m7 |G#m7
But she would die   before I crawled over them.

    |A   Bsus4 B
She is tall - er than I am.

   |E
She knew I wouldn't mind the view there

    |C#m7 |
Or the altitude with a mouthful of air.

G#m7 |A   Bsus4   B ||
She let me down; the doubt came out until the now became later.

Bridge 2

F#m7 |B7
Say   that it isn't so,

           |G#m |C#m   B
How she easily come, how she easy go.

    |A |F#7 |
Please don't tell her 'cause she don't real - ly need to know

Chorus 1

‖E |C♯m7
That I'm crazy like the rest
    |G♯m |A   B
Of us.
           |E |C♯m7
And I'm crazier when I'm next
        |G♯m   A   B   ‖
To her.

Interlude 2   E |C♯m7 |G♯m7 |A   B

Verse 3

      ‖E
So why after the all of everything that came and went,
     |C♯m7 |G♯m7
I care e - nough to still be singing of the bitter end and broken eras.
     |A   Bsus4
I told you I don't.
      B |E
But I am only tryin' to be the best
                           |C♯m7
With my attempt to cure the rest as - sured,
                               |G♯m7
I'll aim to ease the plural hurts of the words reverse
     |A   Bsus4
Psychol - ogy.

Bridge 3

      B‖F♯m7 |B7 |G♯m
That's easier said,
     |C♯m
Easier than done.
      |F♯m7 |B7
Please don't dare to tell her what I've become.
      |G♯m7 |C♯m   B
Please don't mention all the at - tention I have drawn.
      |A |F♯7
Please don't bother, 'cause she'll feel guilty when I'm gone.

Chorus 2

```
                  ‖E                 |C♯m7
Because I'm crazy like the rest
      |G♯m         |A    B
Of us.
            |E                |C♯m7
But I'm crazier when I'm next
      |G♯m            |A      B
To her.
                  |E                 |C♯m7              |G♯m      |A      B
And it's so a - mazing how she's so          self-assured.
      |E                    |C♯m7
But I know she'd hate me if she knew my words.
      |G♯m
Do I hurt anymore?
      |A         B      |E     |C♯m
Do I hurt? Well,  I don't.
         |G♯m7 |A     B      |E        ‖
I don't.                  I don't.
```

90

The Forecast

Words and Music by
Jason Mraz and Eric Hinojosa

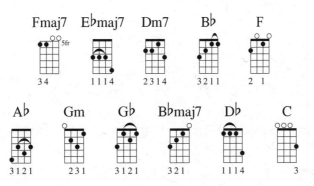

Intro   Fmaj7 |E♭maj7 |Dm7 |B♭ |Fmaj7 |E♭maj7 |Dm7 |B♭

Verse 1

||F |B♭

Well, I heard that it might be raining bed sheets and lover's words.

|F |B♭

Let's throw out   the hotel comforter and hang the "Do   not disturb."

|F |B♭

Sign me up   for the storm. I'll wear my suit for the shower,

|F |B♭

'Cause I'll have you to keep me warm in the coldest hour.

Chorus 1

||A♭   Gm |

And when the darkness falls under your hair,

G♭ |Fmaj7 |B♭maj7

There I'll be.

|A♭ |Gm   G♭ ||

And crazy is the fore - cast   all week.

Interlude 1   Fmaj7 |B♭maj7 |Fmaj7 |B♭maj7

Copyright © 2005 Goo Eyed Music (ASCAP), De Luz Music (ASCAP) and No BS Publishing (ASCAP)
International Copyright Secured   All Rights Reserved

Verse 2

       ‖**F**
Well, every kiss, every hug, is so light on the touch,
    |**B♭**
Deli - cate like a snowflake.
       |**F** |**B♭**
And I can taste, I can taste, I can taste, I can taste you all over my face.
      |**F** |**B♭**
And every - one might find me foolish to not be counting on the sun.
      |**F** |**B♭**
But your mouth is my umbrella now, and I'm holding your tongue.

Chorus 2

       ‖**A♭**
And if the rain should pour,
    Gm | **G♭** |**Fmaj7** |**B♭maj7**
For sure with you I'll be,   ee.
    |**A♭** |**Gm**   **G♭**   ‖
And crazy is the fore - cast all week.

Interlude 2   **Fmaj7** |**B♭maj7**|**Fmaj7** |**B♭maj7**‖

Bridge 1

D♭ |**A♭** |
   There's a good chance   in hail.
C |**F** |
   Like cats and dogs, we'll be fly - ing.
D♭ |**A♭**
   And I'm no weather - man,
     |**C** | ‖
But you are lightning   striking.

Bridge 2

```
        Fmaj7         |Ebmaj7  |Dm7       |Bb
                  La,  la,      la.
                        |Fmaj7               |Ebmaj7
Here comes the sun       and the rain.
              |Dm7                  |Bb        ||
All at once      . now they sing.
```

Verse 3

```
        F                                      |Bb                      |
      In the mist of the morning, pull up a blanket of a cloud
      F                                        |Bb
      And we'll wait for the warning of an - other come down,
            |F                        |Bb                |
Because    the water is healthy for the roses in your cheeks.
      F                             |Bb
      My well holds plenty for penny wishing in your deep end.
```

Chorus 3

```
                  ||Ab
And when the lights go out,
      Gm    |      Gb      |Fmaj7    |Bbmaj7
No doubt,  with you I'll be.
        |Ab              |Gm    Gb      |Fmaj7      |Bbmaj7
Yeah, crazy is the fore  -  cast   all week.
          |Ab
And if the rains should pour,
      Gm   |      Gb      |Fmaj7    |Bbmaj7
For sure  with you I'll be.
          |Ab              |Gm  Gb |Fmaj7        |Bbmaj7      |
Because crazy is the fore   -  cast      all week      long.
Ab              |Gm  Gb |         ||
Crazy is the fore  -  cast.
```

Song for a Friend

Words and Music by
Jason Mraz, Eric Hinojosa, Dennis Morris and Dan Wilson

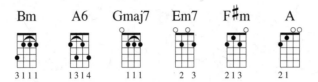

Intro

| Bm | A6 | Gmaj7 | Em7 F#m |

| Bm | A6 | Gmaj7 | Em7 F#m ||

Verse 1

Bm |A6
 "Well, you're magic," he said, but don't let it all go to your head,

   |Gmaj7
'Cause I bet if you all had it all figured out,

   |Em7   F#m
Then you'd never get out of bed.

   |Bm |A6
Well, no doubt of all the thing's that I've read, what he wrote me,

          |Gmaj7 |Em7
Is now sounding like the man I was hoping to be. I keep keeping it real,

      F#m |Em7
'Cause it keeps getting easier, he'll see.

         |A
He's the reason that I'm laugh - ing,

     |Bm   A6 |Gmaj7 |
Even if there's   no one else.

Em7 |A |Bm |A6 |Gmaj7 |Em7 F#m
 He said, you've got to love   yourself.

Copyright © 2005 Goo Eyed Music (ASCAP), De Luz Music (ASCAP), No BS Publishing (ASCAP),
Dirtysick Publishing (ASCAP), Flozkid Music Publishing (ASCAP), Chrysalis Music (ASCAP) and Sugar Lake Music (ASCAP)
All Rights for De Luz Music Administered by No BS Publishing
All Rights for Dirtysick Publishing Administered by Flozkid Music Publishing
All Rights for Chrysalis Music and Sugar Lake Music Administered by BMG Rights Management (US) LLC
International Copyright Secured   All Rights Reserved

Verse 2

          ‖Bm
He said, you shouldn't mum - ble when you speak,
         |A6
But keep your tongue   up in your cheek.
     |Gmaj7
And if you stumble onto something to better,
         |Em7   F♯m
Remember that it's humble that you seek.
    |Bm |A6
You got all   the skill you need; individ - uality.
        |Gmaj7
You've got some - thing; call it gumption,
    |Em7   F♯m
Call it anything you want.

Bridge 1

         ‖Em7 |A
Because when you play the fool now,
        |Bm   A6 |Gmaj7 |
You're only fooling ev - 'ryone else.
Em7 |A |Bm |A6 |
  You're learning to love   yourself.
Gmaj7 |Em7
  Yes, you are,
      F♯m |Bm |A6 |Gmaj7 |Em7   F♯m ‖
You're learning to ...   You, hoo,   you,   hoo.

Bridge 2

Em7 |A |
  There's no price to pay
Em7 |A |
  When you're givin' what you take.
Em7 |A |Bm |A6
  That's why it's easy to thank   you,   you, hoo,
  |Gmaj7 |Em7 F♯m
You,
  |Bm |A6 |Gmaj7 |Em7 F♯m ‖
You,   you,   you.

Verse 3

Bm |A6

Let's say take a break from our day and get back to the old garage,

|Gmaj7 |Em7   F♯m

Because life's too short anyway, but at least it's better than aver - age.

          |Bm

As long as you got me and I got you,

              |A6

You know we got a lot to go around.

          |Gmaj7

I'll be your   friend, your other brother,

       |Em7   F♯m ||

Another love to calm and com - fort you.

Bridge 3

Em7 |A

And I'll keep remind - ing

              |Bm   A6 |Gmaj7 |

If it's the on - ly thing I ever do.

Em7 |A |Bm |A6 |Gmaj7 |Em7 F♯m

I will always love   you,

   |Bm |A6 |Gmaj7 |Em7 F♯m |

You,   you,   you.

Bm |A6 |Gmaj7 |Em7 F♯m ||

Bridge 4

Bm |A6

It's true our love   is true.

       |Gmaj7 |Em7   F♯m

It's you I love,   it's you I love, it's you, it's you   I love.

        |Bm |A6

It's true our love   is true, our love is true. It's you I love.

       |Gmaj7 |Em7   F♯m ||

It's you I love,   it's you I love, it's you, it's you   I love   you, I do.

Interlude   **Bm**   **|A6**   **|Gmaj7**   **|Em7 F♯m** **|**

                Bm   **|A6**   **|Gmaj7**   **|Em7 F♯m** **||**

Chorus 1

Bm   **|A6**
Climb up over the top. Sur - vey the state of the soul.
             |Gmaj7   **|Em7**   **F♯m**   **|**
You've got to find out for yourself whether or not you're tru - ly trying.
Bm   **|A6**
Why not give it a shot? Shake it; take control,
       |Gmaj7
Inevitably wind up finding for yourself
           |Em7   **F♯m**   **||**
All the strengths   you have inside   still rising.

Repeat Chorus 1 (2x)

Chorus 2

Bm   **|A6**
Climb up over the top. Sur - vey the state of the soul.
             |Gmaj7   **|Em7**   **F♯m**   **|**
You've got to find out for yourself whether or not you're tru - ly trying.
Bm   **|A6**
Why not give it a shot? Shake it; take control,
       |Gmaj7
And inevitably wind up and find out for yourself
         |Em7   **F♯m**   **|Bm**   **||**
All the strengths that you have   inside of you.

Make It Mine

Words and Music by
Jason Mraz

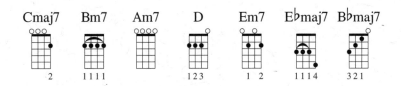

Intro   Cmaj7 | | | |

Verse 1

|Cmaj7 ||Bm7
Wake   up, everyone.
      |Bm7 |Am7
How   can you sleep at a time   like this?
      |Am7 |Cmaj7
Unless the dreamer is the real you.
   |Cmaj7 |Bm7
Lis -   ten to your voice,
      |Bm7 |Am7 |
The one   that tells you to taste   past the tip of your tongue.
               |Cmaj7 |
Leap and the net   will appear.

Chorus 1

                  ||Am7   D |
I don't wanna wake   be - fore
   Bm7 | Em7 |
The dream   is o - ver.
      Am7 | D |
I'm gonna make   it mine.
   Bm7 | Em7 |
Yes, I,   I know it.
      Am7 | D |
I'm gonna make   it mine.
   |Cmaj7 | | | |
Yes, I'll make it all mine.

Copyright © 2008 Goo Eyed Music (ASCAP)
International Copyright Secured   All Rights Reserved

Verse 2

          |Cmaj7   ‖Bm7

I keep my life on a heavy ro - tation,

     |Bm7 |Am7 |

Re - questing that it's lifting you up,   up, up and away

            |Cmaj7 |D |Cmaj7

And over to a table at the Gratitude Cafe.

     |Cmaj7 |Bm7

And I   am finally there.

     |Bm7

And all the angels, they'll be singing,

    |Am7 | |Cmaj7 |D |

Ah, I,   la la la, I, la la la, I,   la la la la, love this.

Chorus 2

                        ‖Am7   D |

Well, I don't wanna break   be - fore

     Bm7| Em7 |

The tour is o - ver.

        Am7 | D |

I'm gonna make it mine.

    Bm7 | Em7|

Yes, I,   I will own it.

       Am7 | D |

I'm gonna make it mine.

  |Cmaj7 | | Em7 D Am7‖

Yes, I'll make it all mine.

Interlude   Am7   D| Bm7| Em7| Am7|

                Am7   D| Bm7| Em7| Am7|

                Am7   D| |Cmaj7 | | | ‖

Bridge

E♭maj7 | |B♭maj7
　　　　　　 Tim - ing's everything,
　　　　|B♭maj7　　　　　|E♭maj7
And this time there's plenty.
　　|E♭maj7　　　　　　|B♭maj7
I　　　am balancing,
　　　|B♭maj7
Care　-　ful and steady,
　　|Am7　　　　　　|　　　　　|D　　　　|
And reveling in energy that everyone's emit - ting.

Outro

　　　　　　　　　　　‖Am7　D　|
Well, I don't wanna wait　　no more.
　　Bm7|　　　　　　Em7　|
Oh, I　　wanna celebrate the whole　world.
　　　　Am7 |　D　　|
I'm gonna make　　it mine.
　　　　Bm7 |　　　　Em7|
Oh, yes, I'm　following your　joy.
　　　Am7 |　D　　|
I'm gonna make　　it mine.
　　Bm7|　　Em7|
Because I,　I am o　-　pen.
　　　Am7 |　D　　|
I'm gonna make　it mine;
　　Bm7 |　　Em7 |
That's why　I will show　it.
　　　Am7 |　　D　|　　Bm7|
I'm gonna make　it all mine.　　　　　Gonna make,

Gonna make, gonna make,
Em7　|　　　　　　　　　　Am7 |　　　D　|
Gonna make it, make it, make it　mine,　　all mine.
　　|Cmaj7　　　　　　|　　　　　‖
Yes, I'll make it all mine.

100

I'm Yours

Words and Music by
Jason Mraz

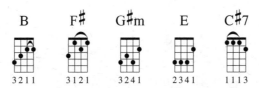

B	F#	G#m	E	C#7
3 2 1 1	3 1 2 1	3 2 4 1	2 3 4 1	1 1 1 3

Intro   B |F# |G#m |E

Verse 1

         ‖B
Well, you done done me in; you bet I felt it.
 |F#
I tried to be chill, but you're so hot that I melted.
 |G#m |E
I fell right through the cracks. Now I'm trying to get back.
         |B
Before the cool done run out, I'll be giving it my bestest,
   |F#
And nothing's going to stop me but divine intervention.
 |G#m |E
I reckon it's again my turn to win some or learn some.

Chorus 1

     ‖B |F# |G#m
But I won't hesi - tate no more, no more.
     |E |B
It cannot wait. I'm yours.
   |F# |G#m |E   ‖
Mm, mm, hmm, mm.

Copyright © 2008 Goo Eyed Music (ASCAP)
International Copyright Secured   All Rights Reserved

Verse 2

     B   **|F#**
Well, open up your mind and see like me.
                             |G#m
Open up your plans and, damn, you're free.
                      |E   **|**
Look into your heart and you'll find love, love, love, love.
B   **|F#**
Listen to the music of the moment; people dance and   sing.
               |G#m
We're just one big family.

                                    |E   **|C#7**
And it's our god-forsaken right to be loved,   loved, loved, loved, loved.

Chorus 2

     ‖B   **|F#**   **|G#m**
So, I won't hesi‑tate no more, no more.
             |E
It cannot wait. I'm sure.
           |B   **|F#**
There's no need to compli‑cate.
          |G#m
Our time is short.
          |E   **‖**
This is our fate. I'm yours.

Interlude

     B   **F#**   **|G#m** **F#**
Scat sing...
                         |E   **|C#7**   **|**
Skooch on over closer, dear,   and I will nibble your ear.   *Scat sing...*
B   **F#**   **|G#m** **F#** **|E**   **|C#7**

Verse 3

      ‖**B**
I've been spending way too long checking my tongue in the mirror
   |**F♯**
And bending over backwards just to try to see it clearer.
  |**G♯m** |**E**
But my breath fogged up the glass, and so I drew a new face and I laughed.
 |**B**
I guess what I'll be saying is there ain't no better reason
   |**F♯**
To rid yourself of vanities and just go with the seasons.
  |**G♯m** |**E**
It's   what we aim to do. Our name is our virtue.

Chorus 3

      ‖**B** |**F♯** |**G♯m**
But I won't hesi‑tate no more, no more.
         |**E** |
It cannot wait. I'm yours.
B |**F♯**
Open up your mind and see like me.
                              |**G♯m**
Open up your plans and, damn, you're free.
                        |**E**
Look into your heart and you'll find that   the sky is yours.
  |**B**
So please don't, please don't, please don't...
      |**F♯** |**G♯m**
There's no need to complicate 'cause our time   is short.
                    |**E** |**C♯7**   ‖
This is, this is, this is our fate. I'm yours.

Outro   **B** |**F♯** |**G♯m** |**E** |**B** ‖
Scat sing...

Lucky

Words and Music by
Jason Mraz, Colbie Caillat and Timothy Fagan

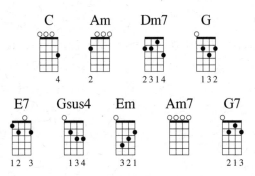

Intro   **C** |

Verse 1
        ‖**C** |**Am**
Do you hear me talking to you?
       |**Dm7** |**G** |**E7**
Across the water, across the deep blue ocean,
     |**Am**
Under the open sky.
    |**Dm7** |**G**
Oh, my,   baby, I'm try - ing.

Verse 2
        ‖**C** |**Am**
Boy, I hear you in my dreams.
    |**Dm7** |**G**
I feel your whisper across the sea.
    |**E7** |**Am**
I keep you with me in my heart.
     |**Dm7** |**G**   **E7**   ‖
You make it easier when life gets hard.

Copyright © 2008 Sony/ATV Music Publishing LLC, Cocomarie Music, Wrunch Time Music and Goo Eyed Music
All Rights on behalf of Sony/ATV Music Publishing LLC, Cocomarie Music and Wrunch Time Music Administered by
Sony/ATV Music Publishing LLC, 8 Music Square West, Nashville, TN 37203
International Copyright Secured   All Rights Reserved

Chorus 1

Am |Dm7 |G
     Lucky I'm in   love with my best friend,
               |C |Am
Lucky to have been where I have been.
          |Dm7 |Gsus4 |G |
Lucky to be coming home a - gain.
C |Am |Em |G ||
Oo,   oo.

Bridge

Dm7 |Am7 |G
They don't know how long it takes,
             |Dm7 |
Waiting for a love like this.
Dm7 |Am7 |
Every time we say goodbye,
G |Dm7
  I wish we had one more kiss.
 |Dm7 |Am7 |G Am7 |G7 ||
I'll wait for you, I promise you I will.   I'm

Chorus 2

Am7 |Dm7 |G7
     Lucky I'm in   love with my best friend,
              |C |Am7
Lucky to have been where I have been.
         |Dm7 |Gsus4 |G |
Lucky to be coming home a - gain.
Am7 |Dm7 |G7
     Lucky we're in   love in every way,
            |C |Am7
Lucky to have stayed where we have stayed.
         |Dm7 |Gsus4 |G
Lucky to be coming home some - day.

Verse 3

```
              ‖C                    |Am
And so I'm sailing through the    sea
         |Dm7              |G
To an island where we'll meet.
                    |E7        |Am
You'll hear the music fill the air.
            |Dm7 |G
I'll put a flower in your hair.
```

Verse 4

```
              ‖C                 |Am
Though the breezes through the trees
            |Dm7            |G
Move so pretty, you're all I see.
         |E7             |Am
As the world keeps spinning 'round,
      |Dm7         |G        E7      ‖
You hold me right here, right now.
```

Repeat Chorus 2

Outro

```
     C     |Am    |Em     |G        |
     Oo,          oo.
     C     |Am    |Em     |G      |C      ‖
     Oo,          oo.
```

Butterfly

Words and Music by
Jason Mraz

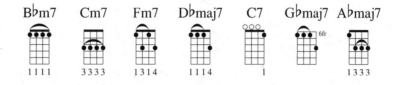

Bbm7 Cm7 Fm7 Dbmaj7 C7 Gbmaj7 Abmaj7

Intro

Bbm7 Cm7   Fm7 | |Bbm7 Cm7   Fm7 | |

Bbm7 Cm7 | ||

Verse 1

Fm7 | |Bbm7
    I'm taking a moment, just imag - ining that I'm dancing with you.
      |Bbm7 |Cm7
I'm your pole and all you're wearing is your shoes.
     |Cm7 |Dbmaj7
You got soul; you know what to do to turn   me on
          |C7 |
Until I write a song   about you.
Fm7 | |Bbm7
    And you have your own engaging style.
      |Bbm7 |Cm7
And you've got the knack to vivify.
      |Cm7
And you make my slacks a little tight;
      |Dbmaj7
You may unfast   -   en them if you like.
    |C7
That's if you crash and spend the night.

Copyright © 2008 Goo Eyed Music (ASCAP)
International Copyright Secured   All Rights Reserved

Chorus 1

‖B♭m7   Cm7   Fm7|

But you don't fold, you don't fade, you got ev - 'rything you need,

|B♭m7 Cm7   Fm7|

·Especially me.   Sister, you've got it all.

|B♭m7   Cm7

You make the call   to make my day.

|Fm7

In your mes - sage say my name.

|B♭m7   Cm7 |Fm7 |B♭m7 Cm7 |

Your talk is all the talk. Sister, you've got it all.

Fm7 |B♭m7 Cm7 |Fm7 |

    You've got it all.

Verse 2

‖B♭m7 |

Curl your upper lip   up and let me look around.

Cm7 |Fm7 |

   Ride your tongue along your bot - tom lip and bite down.

D♭maj7 |G♭maj7

   And bend your back and ask those hips if I can touch.

|C7 |

'Cause they're the perfect jumping off point, getting closer

Pre-Chorus 1

‖Fm7 |B♭m7

To your butter - fly. You float on by.

|Cm7 |Fm7

Oh, kiss me with your eyelashes   tonight.

|D♭maj7 |G♭maj7

Or Eskimo your nose real close   to mine.

|C7 |

And let's mood the lights and finally make it right.

Chorus 2

     ‖Bbm7   Cm7   Fm7 |
But you don't fold, you don't fade, you got ev - 'rything you need,

           |Bbm7 Cm7   Fm7 |
Especially me.   Sister, you've got it all.

          |Bbm7   Cm7
You make the call   to make my day.

        |Fm7
In your mes - sage say my name.

      |Bbm7   Cm7 |Fm7
Your talk is all the talk. Sister, you've got it all.

       |Bbm7   Cm7 |Fm7
You've got it all,   you've got it all, you've got it all.

       |Bbm7   Cm7 |Fm7
You've got it all,   you've got it all, you've got it all.

       |Bbm7   Cm7 |
You've got it all.

Fm7 |Bbm7   Cm7 |Fm7 | ‖
   You've got it a - a - ll.

Bridge

Bbm7 | |Dbmaj7 |
Doll, I need to see you pull your knee socks up.

Dbmaj7 |Abmaj7 | |C7
Let me feel you upside down, slide in, slide out, slide over here.

  |C7   ‖
Climb   into my mouth now, child.

Interlude

Fm7 Bbm7 |Cm7 Fm7 |Dbmaj7 Gbmaj7 |C7 |
Scat sing...
Fm7 Bbm7 |Cm7 Fm7 |Dbmaj7 Gbmaj7 |C7

Pre-Chorus 2

```
 ‖Fm7                        |B♭m7
Butter - fly, well, you landed on     my mind.
            |Cm7                                    |Fm7
Damn right you landed on my ear and then you crawled     inside.
            |D♭maj7                        |G♭maj7
And now        I see you perfectly behind        closed eyes.
            |C7                                    |
I want to fly with you. And I don't want to lie to you.
```

Chorus 3

```
                                    ‖B♭m7          Cm7
'Cause I, 'cause I can't recall     a better day,
                            |Fm7
Sun coming to shine     on the occasion.
            |B♭m7          Cm7            |Fm7
You're an o - pen-minded lady; you've got it all.
            |B♭m7    Cm7                  |Fm7
And I never forget a face, 'cept maybe my own.
                              |B♭m7          Cm7            |Fm7
I have my days. Let's face the fact     here, it's you who's got it all.
            |B♭m7          Cm7
You know that for - tune favors the brave.
            |Fm7
Well, let me get paid while I make you breakfast.
            |B♭m7          Cm7            |Fm7
The rest     is up to you.   You make the call.
            |B♭m7          Cm7
You make the call     to make my day.
            |Fm7
In your mes - sage say my name.
            |B♭m7          Cm7            |Fm7
Your talk is all the talk. Sister, you've got it all.
```

Outro

‖**N.C.** |

I can't recall   a better day, sun coming to shine on the occasion.

|

Hey, sophis - ticated lady.

| |**B♭m7**   **Cm7** |**Fm7**

Oh, you've got it all,   you've got it all, you've got it all.

         |**B♭m7**   **Cm7** |**Fm7**

You've got it all,   you've got it all, you've got it all.

         |**B♭m7**   **Cm7** |**Fm7**

You've got it all,   you've got it all, you've got it all.

         |**B♭m7**   **Cm7** |**Fm7**

You've got it all,   you've got it all, you've got it all.

         |**B♭m7** **Cm7** |

Hey! You've got it all.   Woo!

Fm7 |**B♭m7** **Cm7** |

   You've got, you, you've got it all.   Hey!

Fm7 |**B♭m7** **Cm7**

   You gots, you gots, you gots, you got it all.

  |**Fm7** |**B♭m7** **Cm7** |

Oh!   You've got, you've it all.   Hey!

Fm7   **Cm7**|**B♭m7** |

  But - ter - fly,

C7 |**Tacet** |**Fm7**   ‖

Baby, well, you got it all.

Live High

Words and Music by
Jason Mraz

A	C#m7	Cm7	Bm7	Dm7	D	Dmaj7	F#m	Bm
21	3333	2222	1111	2314	123	1114	213	3111

Intro   A |C#m7   Cm7 |Bm7 |Dm7

‖A

Verse 1   I try to picture the girl
|C#m7
Through a look - ing glass
|D
And see her as a car - bon atom.
|Dm7
See her eyes   and stare back at them.
|A
See that girl
|C#m7
As her own new world.
|D |Dm7 |
Though a home   is on the surface, she is still a universe.
A |C#m7
   Glory God or Goddess peek - ing through the blinds.
|D
Are we all   here standing naked,
|Dm7 |A
Taking guesses at the actual date and time?
|C#m7
Oh my! Justify - ing reasons why
|D |Dm7
Is an ab - solutely insane resolu - tion to live by.

Copyright © 2008 Goo Eyed Music (ASCAP)
International Copyright Secured   All Rights Reserved

Chorus 1

‖**A**
Live high.

|**C♯m7**
Live might - y.

Cm7 |**Bm7** |
Live   righteously.

Dm7
   Taking it easy.

|**A**
Live high.

|**C♯m7**
Live might - y.

Cm7 |**Bm7** |**Dm7**
Live   righteously.

‖**A**

Verse 2   And try to picture the man

|**C♯m7** |**D**
To always have an open hand and see him as a giv - ing tree.

|**Dm7** |**A**
See him as mat - ter. Matter of fact, he's not a beast.

|**C♯m7** |**D**
No, not the dev - il either. Always a good deed doer.

|**Dm7** |**A**
And it's laughter that we're making after all.

|**C♯m7**
The Call of the Wild is still an or - der nationwide.

|**D** |**Dm7** |
In the or - der of the primates, all our pol - itics are too late.

A |**C♯m7**
   Oh my, the congrega - tion in my mind

|**D** |**Dm7**   ‖
Is this as - sembly singing of gratitude, practicing their loving for you.

                              A
Chorus 2   Live high.
                                 |**C♯m7**
                   Live might   -   y.
                   Cm7 |**Bm7** |**Dm7**
                   Live   righteously.   Mm.

                   Taking it easy.
                        |**A**
                   Live high.
                                 |**C♯m7**
                   Live might   -   y.

                        Cm7|**Bm7** |**Dm7**
                   Oh, live   righteously.

                                 ‖**Dmaj7**
Bridge   Sing it out.
                                 |**Dm7**
                   And just take   it easy,
                       |**C♯m7** |**F♯m**
                   And celebrate the malleable real - ity.
                            |**Bm**
                   You see, nothing is ever as it seems.
                            |**Dm7** | ‖
                   Yeah, this life is but a dream.

Outro

```
A                                          |C♯m7                Cm7 |Bm7
        Lift me up to Thee, Almight   -   y!
                                           |Dm7                      |A
Raise your hands and start acknowl  -  edging        He.
                          |C♯m7
If you're living it right   -   eously,
                               Cm7      |Bm7              |Dm7
Then you're tak - ing the eas  -  y way.
              |A
Live high,     live high.
              |C♯m7
Live might   -   y, mighty, mighty.
    Cm7    |Bm7                 |Dm7
Oh,     live     righteously.
                            |A
Takin' it easy, live high.     (Live High!)
              |C♯m7
Live might   -   y. (Lift me up to Thee!)
    Cm7      |Bm7                             |Dm7
Oh, live right  -  eously. (Living Righteously.)
                                    |A
Just take… Just, just takin' it eas - y. (Live High!)
              |C♯m7
Oh, live might   -   y, mighty.
    Cm7    |Bm7                      |Dm7
Oh,    live righteously. And sing it out.
              |A
Just take it eas - y.
                |C♯m7
I say Live High!
    Cm7 |Bm7                |Dm7                       ||
Oh! Live   Righteously!          Just take it easy.
```

Love for a Child

Words and Music by
Jason Mraz, Martin Terefe and Sacha Skarbek

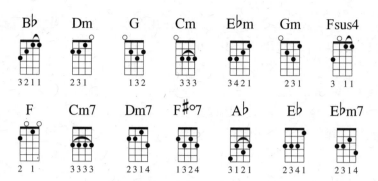

Intro

Bb |Dm |G |Cm |

Cm Ebm |Bb Dm   Gm |Cm |Fsus4   F

||Bb

Verse 1
There's a picture on my kitchen wall,
    |Dm
Looks like Jesus and his friends involved.
    |G |Cm
There's a party getting started in the yard.
    |Cm   Ebm |Bb   F   Gm
And there's a couple getting steamy in the car parked in the drive.
    |Cm |Fsus4   F
Was I too young to see this with my eyes?

Copyright © 2008 Goo Eyed Music (ASCAP), Sony/ATV Music Publishing UK Ltd., Key Red Ltd. and Universal Music Publishing Ltd.
All Rights for Sony/ATV Music Publishing UK Ltd. and Key Red Ltd.
Administered by Sony/ATV Music Publishing LLC, 8 Music Square West, Nashville, TN 37203
All Rights for Universal Music Publishing Ltd. in the U.S. and Canada Controlled and Administered by Universal - Songs Of PolyGram International, Inc.
International Copyright Secured   All Rights Reserved

Verse 2

```
                     ‖ B♭
And by the pool that night, apparently
         | Dm
The chemicals weren't mixed properly.
         | G                                      | Cm
You hit your head and then forgot your name.
               | Cm            E♭m          | B♭  F      Gm
And then you woke up at the bot - tom by the drain.
                   | Cm                     | Fsus4    F        ‖
And now your altitude and memory's a shame.
```

Chorus

```
      B♭            Cm7      | Dm7            Cm7
   What about taking this   empty cup and filling it up
         | B♭            Cm7
With a little bit more of innocence.
  | Dm7                Cm7
I haven't had enough; it's probably because
                 | B♭          F♯°7      | Gm            A♭               |
When you're young, it's o - kay to be    easily ignored.
 E♭                       | E♭m7                    | B♭            ‖
   I'd like to believe it was all about love for a child.
```

Verse 3

```
  B♭                                | Dm
   When the house was left in sham - bles,
                   | G                              | Cm
Who was there to han - dle all the broken bits of glass?
         | Cm          E♭m                |
Was it Mom who put my dad out on his ass,
 B♭        F          Gm
   Or the other way a - round?
         | Cm                          | Fsus4   F        ‖
Well, I'm far too old to care about that now.
```

Repeat Chorus

Bridge

Ab   Cm |Bb   Dm
It's kinda nice   to work the floor   since the divorce.

               |Ab   Cm |Bb
I've been enjoy - ing both my Christmases and my birthday cakes.

       |Ab   Cm |Bb   Dm
And taking drugs and making love at far too young an age.

        |Ab
And they never checked to see my grades.

     |F | ||
What a fool I'd be to start complain - ing now.

Repeat Chorus

     |Ebm7 |Bb ||
It was all about love.

Details in the Fabric
(Sewing Machine)

Words and Music by
Jason Mraz and Dan Wilson

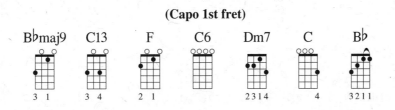

(Capo 1st fret)

Bbmaj9   C13   F   C6   Dm7   C   Bb

Intro

| Bbmaj9 | | | C13 | | |

| Bbmaj9 | | | C13 | |

Verse 1

‖ Bbmaj9 |
Calm   down,

| C13 |
Deep   breaths,

| Bbmaj9 |
And get your   -   self dressed

| C13 |
In - stead

| Bbmaj9
Of running around

| Bbmaj9 | C13
And pulling on your threads and

| C13
Breaking yourself up.

| Bbmaj9
If it's a bro   -   ken part, replace it.

| Bbmaj9
If it's a broken arm, then brace it.

| N.C. |
If it's a broken heart, then face it.

Copyright © 2008 Goo Eyed Music (ASCAP), Chrysalis Music (ASCAP) and Sugar Lake Music (ASCAP)
All Rights for Chrysalis Music and Sugar Lake Music Administered by BMG Rights Management (US) LLC
International Copyright Secured   All Rights Reserved

Chorus 1

‖ **F**
And hold your own,

|**C6** |**Dm7** |
Know your name, and go your own way.

|**F**
Hold your own,

|**C6** |**Dm7**
Know your own name, and go your own way.

|**C** |**B♭** |
And every   -   thing

|**C** | ‖
Will be fine.

Repeat Intro

Verse 2

‖**B♭maj9** |
Hang   on.

|**C13** |
Help is on   the way.

|**B♭maj9** |
Stay   strong.

|**C13** |
I'm doing   everything.

Chorus 2

‖**F**
Hold your own,

|**C6** |**Dm7** |
Know your name, and go your own way.

|**F**
Hold your own,

|**C6** |**Dm7**
Know your own name, and go your own way.

|**C** |**B♭** |**C** |**B♭**
And every   -   thing, every - thing will be fine.

|**C**
Every - thing.

Bridge

```
         || F
Are  the  details  in  the  fabric?
            | C6
Are  there  things  that  make  you  panic?
          | Dm7                           |
Are  your  thoughts  results  of  static  cling?
          | F
Are  there  things  that  make  you  blow?
          | C6
Hell,  no  reason.  Go  on  and  scream.
          | Dm7                      | C              | Bb
If  you're  shocked  it's  just  the  fault  of  faulty  manufacturing.
      | C            | Bb
Every - thing  will  be  fine.
      | C              | Bb
Every - thing  in  no  time    at  all.
      | C             |
Every - thing.
```

|| F
Chorus 3   Hold your own,

                              | C6 | Dm7 |
               Know your name,   go your own way.

                      | F
               Are the details in the fabric?

                      | C6
               Are there things that make you panic?

                      | Dm7 |
               Are your thoughts results of static cling?

                      | F
               Are the details in the fabric?

                      | C6
               Are there things that make you panic?

                  | Dm7 |
               Is it Mother Nature's sewing machine?

                      | F
               Are there things that make you blow?

                      | C6
               Hell, no reason. Go on and scream.

                  | Dm7 | C | Bb
               If you're shocked it's just the fault of faulty manufacturing.

                  | C | Bb
               Every - thing will be fine.

                  | C | Bb
               Every - thing in no time   at all.

                      | C | ||
               Hearts will hold.

Outro   Bbmaj9 | | C13 | |

            Bbmaj9 | | C13 | |

            Bbmaj9 | | C13 | ||

Coyotes

Words and Music by
Jason Mraz

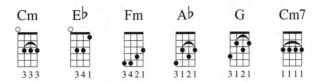

Cm   Eb   Fm   Ab   G   Cm7

333   341   3421   3121   3121   1111

Verse 1

Cm
    I'm sipping coffee at a quarter to two.
|**Eb** |
A - wake and I'm dialing and my mind's running to you.
Fm
No wonder I'm a one-woman man.
Ab   **G**
She keeps my heart in a jar   on a nightstand.
Cm
I should tell her that she couldn't be more
Eb
Opposite than a foot in the door.
Fm
There's no one else I would rather go out with.
|**Ab**   **G**
It's hell when I see them standing there.
Cm
Me and my mouth, we don't mean to be rushing.
Eb
We talk about thee freely 'cause we crushing.
Fm
I'm gonna shake both sides of the butt, yeah.
Ab   **G**
Theoretically. Yes. Ain't we lucky?

Copyright © 2008 Goo Eyed Music (ASCAP)
International Copyright Secured   All Rights Reserved

Pre-Chorus 1

```
Fm                                     |Cm7                        |
    And when the coyotes, they sing        in the park,
Fm                              |Cm7                  |
    Is when the city life starts falling for the sea.
Fm
    Winding roads are winding down
        |Cm7                                    |
And the     flying men will hit the ground.
Fm
    Every notion is closer to touching.
    |G                                          ||
The coyotes sing when they call on your loving.
```

Interlude 1

```
Cm        |E♭        |Fm        |A♭    G    ||
```

Chorus 1

```
Cm
    We're coming back for more.
                 |E♭
You know why      we're coming for you.
              |Fm          |
You know we should be,
A♭                      G       |
    We should be togeth - er.
Cm                                |E♭
    Cuz once we rock, we won't     wanna stop.
      |Fm                        |A♭                  G           |
Not to - day or tomorrow. Not to - day or tomorrow,   oh, no.
Cm
    You better lock your doors.
                 |E♭
You know why,   'cause we want you.
       |Fm                |A♭    G       ||
Cuz we like you a lotta.
```

Interlude 2

```
Fm        |Cm        |Fm        |G        |        ||
```

Verse 2

Cm |
   I wish the wild was alive like you.

E♭ |
   I wish the wind would blow me through

Fm |
   Another opportunity to approach you,

A♭   G |
   Another telepathic rendezvous.

Cm |
   I wish you well with your weapon of jargon.

E♭ |
   You've got a double-sided lexicon.

Fm
   I gotta try to keep your attention,

  |A♭   G |
Gotta write using less e - moticons.

Cm |
   Gotta figure out the snooze alarm.

E♭ |
   I wanna lay in your place till dawn.

Fm
   I wanna play in the park, come on.

   |A♭   G | |N.C. ‖
Now let me see your other upper echelon.

Pre-Chorus 2

Fm |Cm7 |
   And when the coyotes es - cape to New York,

Fm |Cm7 |
   Then the city life has crum - bled to the sea.

Fm |Cm7
   And the girls will fall to the lost and found,

              |
The flying men will hit the ground.

Fm
   Every notion is closer to touching.

 |G |Cm |E♭ |Fm
The coyotes sing when they feast on your loving.

   |A♭   G   ‖
I'm a coyote and I got a taste for your loving.

Chorus 2

Cm
    We're coming back for more.

        |Eb
You know why   we're coming for you.

      |Fm |
You know we should be,

Ab   G |
    We should be togeth - er.

Cm |Eb
    Because once we rock, we won't   wanna stop.

    |Fm |Ab   G |
Not to - day or tomorrow. Not to - day or tomorrow, oh, no.

Cm |Eb
    Because once we rock, we won't   wanna stop.

    |Fm |Ab   G |
Not to - day or tomorrow. Oh,   mm.

Cm
    We're coming back for more.

        |Eb
You know why   we're coming for you.

     |Fm |
You know we should be,

Ab   G |
    We should be togeth - er.

Cm |Eb
    Cuz once we rock, we won't   wanna stop.

    |Fm |Ab   G |Cm ||
Not to - day or tomorrow.

Only Human

Words and Music by
Jason Mraz and Sacha Skarbek

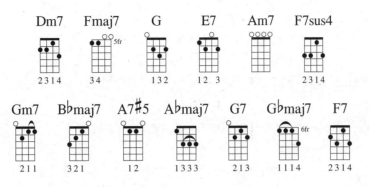

Intro   **Dm7** | | | ‖

Verse 1
   Dm7
    Squirrel in the tree, is he watching me?
        |**Dm7** |
Does he give a damn? Does he care who I am?
Dm7
    I'm just a man. Is that all I am?
        |**Dm7**
Are my man - ners misinterpreted? Words are only human.
      |**Dm7** | ‖
I'm hu - man.

Copyright © 2008 Goo Eyed Music (ASCAP) and Universal Music Publishing Ltd.
All Rights for Universal Music Publishing Ltd. in the U.S. and Canada Controlled and Administered by Universal - Songs Of PolyGram International, Inc.
International Copyright Secured   All Rights Reserved

Verse 2

    Dm7

Murderous crow, hey, what you know?

    | **Dm7** |

What'cha rav - ing about? What'cha hold in your toes?

Dm7

Is that a twig? Are you a dove of peace?

    | **Dm7** |

Black dove   undercover with another puzzle piece.

Dm7

Are you a riddle to solve all along

    | **Dm7**

Or am I over-thinking thoughts? I'm human after all,

    |**Dm7** | ||

Only hu - man.   Made of flesh, made of sand, made of hu - man.

Pre-Chorus

    Fmaj7   **G** |

The planet's talking about a revolution.

E7   **Am7**

The natural laws ain't got   no constitution.

    |**Dm7**

They've   got a right to live their own life.

      |**E7**

But we keep paving over paradise.

Chorus 1

              ||**Dm7** |**F7sus4**

'Cause we're only hu - man.   Oh yes, we are.

    |**Gm7**

Only hu - man.

              |**B♭maj7**   **A7♯5**

If it's our only excuse,   how do you think we'll keep on

    |**Dm7** |**F7sus4**

Being only hu - man?   Oh yes, we are.

    |**Gm7** |**B♭maj7**   **A7♯5** ||

Only hu - man.   So far,   so far.

Interlude   **Dm7** | | | ||

Dm7

Verse 3   Up in the major's tree,

                           | **Dm7** |

The one he planted back when he was just a boy back in 1923.

Dm7

     Thirty meters and a foot, take a look,

     | **Dm7** |

Take a climb. What you'll find is the product of a seed.

Dm7 |

     The seed is sown; all alone it grows above, with a heart of love,

          | **Dm7**

A sharpened shelter of   the ani - mals of land

          | **Dm7** ||

And cold weather breath - ing. We're all breathing.

Repeat Pre-Chorus

Repeat Chorus 1

               || **B♭maj7**   **A7♯5**

Bridge   And this place, it will out - live me.

     | **A♭maj7**   **G7**

Be - fore I get to heaven I'll climb   that tree.

     | **G♭maj7**   **F7**

And I will have to give my thanks

     | **G♭maj7**   **A♭maj7** | **B♭maj7**

For giving me the branch to swing   on.

          A7♯5 | **A♭maj7**   **G7**

If I ev - er fall   in love,

     | **G♭maj7**   **F7**

I'll hope to get myself a ba - by.

     | **G♭maj7**   **A♭maj7**

I will let my children have their way.

Chorus 2

        ‖**Dm7** |**F7sus4**
Because we're only hu - man.   Oh yes, we are.

    |**Gm7**
Only hu - man.

    |**B♭maj7**   **A7♯5** |**Dm7** |**F7sus4** |**Gm7**
So far,   so far.

    |**B♭maj7**   **A7♯5**   ‖
So far,   so far.

Outro   **Dm7** | | | ‖

The Dynamo of Volition

Words and Music by
Jason Mraz

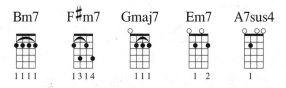

Bm7   F#m7   Gmaj7   Em7   A7sus4

‖**Bm7**

Verse 1   I got the dyna - mo of volition, the p-pole position,

|**F#m7**   **Gmaj7**
Auto - matic transmission with 1 - low emissions.

|**Bm7** |**F#m7**   **Gmaj7**
I'm a brand-new addition to the old edition with the love uncondition - al.

|**Bm7** |**F#m7**
And I'm a drama abolitionist, damn, no opposition to my proposition.

Gmaj7
Half of a man, half magician.

|**Bm7**
Half a politician holding the mic like ammunition,

|**F#m7**   **Gmaj7**
And my vision is as simple as light.

|**Bm7**
Ain't no reason we should be in a fight, no demolition.

|**F#m7**   **Gmaj7**
Get to vote, get to say what you like, procreation.

|**Bm7** |
Compo - sitions already written by themselves.

F#m7   **Gmaj7** |
Heck is for the people not believing in gosh.

Copyright © 2008 Goo Eyed Music (ASCAP)
International Copyright Secured   All Rights Reserved

**Chorus 1**

|| Bm7

Good job.

|F♯m7   Gmaj7

Get 'em up way high. Gimme, gimme that high   five.

|Bm7

Good   times.

|F♯m7   Gmaj7

Get 'em way down low. Gimme, gimme that low   dough.

|Bm7

Good   God.

|F♯m7   Gmaj7

Bring 'em back again. Gimme, gimme that high   ten.

|Bm7 Tacet |F♯m7   Gmaj7 ||

You're the best definition of good inten - tions.

**Bridge 1**

Em7 |F♯m7 |Gmaj7

I do not answer the call if I do not know who is calling.

|A7sus4 |

I guess the whole point of it all is that we never know really.

Em7 |F♯m7 |Gmaj7

I'm trying to keep with the Joneses while waiting for guns and the roses

|A7sus4 |Bm7 |

To finish what we all sup - pose is gonna be the shit, as - suming.

F♯m7   Gmaj7 |Bm7 |F♯m7   Gmaj7

Verse 2

‖**Bm7 Tacet** |**F♯m7**
Oh, fists knock bumping and wrists locked twisting up a rizla.
Gmaj7 |**Bm7** |**F♯m7**
Kid Icarus on the tran - sistor. Nintendo been giving me the blister.
Gmaj7 |**Bm7**
I bend over, take it in the kisser.

                           |**F♯m7**
My best friends are hitting on my   sister.
  Gmaj7 |**Bm7**
I try to tell 'em that they still a wisher,
                      |**F♯m7**
'Cause she already got herself a mister.
       Gmaj7 |**Bm7**
And be - sides, that's gross, don't wanna dis her.
    |**F♯m7**   **Gmaj7** |
A-d-d-d-d-d-didn't I say, didn't I say.

Chorus 2

       ‖**Bm7**
Good job.

                     |**F♯m7**   **Gmaj7**
Get 'em up way high. Gimme, gimme that high   five.
    |**Bm7**
Good   times.
                     |**F♯m7**   **Gmaj7**
Get 'em way down low. Gimme, gimme that low   dough.
    |**Bm7**
Good   God.
                     |**F♯m7**   **Gmaj7**
Bring 'em back again. Gimme, gimme that high   ten.
   |**Bm7 Tacet** |**F♯m7**   **Gmaj7**   ‖
You're the best definition of good versus evil.

Verse 3

    Bm7   **|F♯m7**
        I do not keep up with statistics.

    Gmaj7   **|Bm7**
I   do not sleep without a mistress.

           |F♯m7   **Gmaj7**   **|Bm7**
I do not eat unless it's fixed with some   kind of sweet, like a licorice.

             |F♯m7
My home is deep inside the mystics.

    Gmaj7   **|Bm7**
I'm   known to keep digging on ex - istence.

             |F♯m7
I'm holding in the heat like a fish stick.

Gmaj7
My phone, it beeps

Bridge 2

           ‖Em7
Because I missed it.

           |F♯m7   **|Gmaj7**
I do not answer the call if I do not know who is calling.

               |A7sus4
I'm making no sense of it all. Say, can I get a witness?

Em7   **|F♯m7**   **|Gmaj7**
   I'm only a boy in a   story, just a hallucina - tory

              |A7sus4
Tripping on nothing there is, living in the wilderness.

Em7   **|F♯m7**   **|Gmaj7**
   With a tiger spot on my   back, living life of a   cat.

           |A7sus4
I just want to relax   here and write another rap tune.

Em7   **|F♯m7**   **|Gmaj7**
   Driving off on your blind man's bike, you can say just what you like;

  |A7sus4   **|Bm7**   **|F♯m7**   **Gmaj7**
Oh, nothing can stop you.

Bm7   **|F♯m7**   **Gmaj7**

Chorus 3

     ‖Bm7
Good job.

                            |F♯m7   **Gmaj7**
Get 'em up way high. Gimme, gimme that high   five.

     |Bm7
Good   times.

                         |F♯m7   **Gmaj7**
Get 'em way down low. Gimme, gimme that low   dough.

     |Bm7
Good   God.

                        |F♯m7   **Gmaj7**
Bring 'em back again. Gimme, gimme that high   ten.

     |Bm7 Tacet
You're the best, you're the best, you're the best, you're the best,

     |F♯m7   **Gmaj7**
You're the best, you're the best, you're the best.

Chorus 4

     ‖Bm7
Good job.

                         |F♯m7   **Gmaj7**
Get 'em up way high. Gimme, gimme that high   five.

     |Bm7
Good   times.

                         |F♯m7   **Gmaj7**
Get 'em way down low. Gimme, gimme that low   dough.

     |Bm7
Good   God.

                        |F♯m7   **Gmaj7**
Bring 'em back again. Gimme, gimme that high   ten.

     |Bm7 Tacet   **|F♯m7**   **Gmaj7**
You're the best definition of good inten - tions.

     |Bm7 Tacet   **|F♯m7**   **Gmaj7**
You're the best definition of good inten - tions.

     |Bm7 Tacet   **|F♯m7**   **Gmaj7**
You're the best definition of good inten - tions.

       |Tacet Bm7   **|F♯m7**   **Gmaj7**   **‖**
You're the best   around.

If It Kills Me

Words and Music by
Jason Mraz, Martin Terefe and Sacha Skarbek

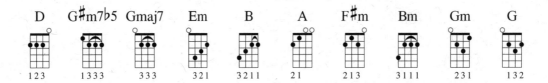

Verse 1

D |G#m7♭5   Gmaj7 |
Hello.   Tell me you know.   Yeah, you figured me out.

D |G#m7♭5 Gmaj7 |
Something   gave it away.

D |G#m7♭5   Gmaj7 |
It would be such a beautiful mo   -   ment to see the look on your face,

D |G#m7♭5   Gmaj7 |
To know that   I know that you know   now.

Em |B   Em   B
And baby, that's a case of my wish - ful   think - ing.

     |A |
You   know   nothing.

D |G#m7♭5   Gmaj7 |
Well, you and I, why, we go car   -   rying on for hours   on end.

D |G#m7♭5 |Gmaj7   Tacet ||
We get along much bet   -   ter than you   and your boyfriend.

Copyright © 2008 Goo Eyed Music (ASCAP), Sony/ATV Music Publishing UK Ltd., Key Red Ltd. and Universal Music Publishing Ltd.
All Rights for Sony/ATV Music Publishing UK Ltd. and Key Red Ltd.
Administered by Sony/ATV Music Publishing LLC, 8 Music Square West, Nashville, TN 37203
All Rights for Universal Music Publishing Ltd. in the U.S. and Canada Controlled and Administered by Universal - Songs Of PolyGram International, Inc.
International Copyright Secured   All Rights Reserved

Chorus 1

>   D |F♯m

D | F♯m

Well, all I really want do is love you.

| Bm

A kind much closer than friends use,

| Gm |

But I still can't say it after all we've been through.

D | F♯m

And all I really want from you is to feel me

| Bm

As the feeling inside keeps build - ing.

| Gm |

And I will find a way to you if it kills me, if it kills me.

D | Gm ||

Verse 2

D | G♯m7♭5 Gmaj7 |

How long can I go on like this, wishing to kiss you

D | G♯m7♭5 Gmaj7 |

Before I rightly explode?

D | G♯m7♭5

Well, this double life I lead isn't health - y for me;

Gmaj7 |

In fact, it makes me nervous.

D | G♯m7♭5 Gmaj7 |

If I get caught I could be risking it all.

Em | B Em B | A ||

'Cause maybe there's a lot that I miss in case I'm wrong.

Chorus 2

```
            D                          |F♯m
      All I really want do is love        you.
                                     |Bm
A kind much closer than friends       use,
                          |Gm                      |
But I still can't say it after all    we've been through.
            D                                   |F♯m
      And all I really want from you is to feel      me
                               |Bm
As the feeling inside keeps build - ing.
                                    |Gm
And I will find a way to you if it kills    me, if it kills me,
            |D                |Gm        ||
If it kills  me, ah.
```

Bridge

```
      Em
      If I should be so bold,
   |B                    Em
I'd ask you to hold my heart    in your hand;
   |B                              Em   B        |A
I'd tell you from the start how I've longed   to be your man.
      |A           Tacet                                |
But I never said a word. I guess I've gone and missed my chance again.
D          |F♯m        |G        |Gm           ||
```

Chorus 3

```
            D                                    |F♯m
      Well, all I really want do is love      you.
                                      |Bm
A kind much closer than friends      use,
                                |Gm                          |
But I still can't say it after all    we've been through.
D                                            |F♯m
   And all I really want from you is to feel       me
                                    |Bm
As the feeling inside keeps build - ing.

                                        |Gm
And I will find a way to you if it kills    me, if it kills me,
              |D             |F♯m
If it kills  me.
                        |Bm                |Gm                |
Oh, I think it might kill me.
D                                              |F♯m
   And all I really want to do is to feel      you.
                                    |B
Yeah, the feeling inside keeps build - ing.
                                  |Gm
I'll find a way to you if it kills    me, if it kills me.
              |D           |Gm          |D              ||
It might kill  me.
```

A Beautiful Mess

Words and Music by
Jason Mraz, Mona Tavakoli, Chaska Potter, Mai Bloomfield and Becky Gebhard

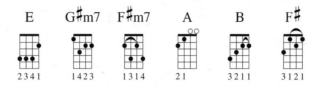

Intro   E |G♯m7 |F♯m7 |A   B |

       E |G♯m7 |F♯m7 |A   B

            ‖ E |

Verse 1
You've got the best of both worlds;

G♯m7 |F♯m7
    You're the kind of girl who can take down a man

 |A   B
And lift him back up a - gain.

       |E |
You are   strong but you're needy.

G♯m7
Humble but you're greedy,

   |F♯m7 |A   B
And based on your body language and shoddy cursive I've been read - ing,

   |E
Your style is quite selective,

      |G♯m7
Though your mind is rather reckless.

   |F♯m7 |A   B   ‖
Well, I guess it just suggests that this is just what happi - ness is.

Copyright © 2008 Goo Eyed Music (ASCAP) and Raining Jane (ASCAP)
International Copyright Secured   All Rights Reserved

Pre-Chorus 1

```
A                    |                    |B     |        |
         And what a beautiful mess this is.
A              |              |B        |
         It's like  we're picking up trash in    dresses.
```

Chorus 1

```
        ‖E                      |G♯m7                    |
Well, it    kind of hurts when the      kind of words you write
F♯m7                      |A            B
     Kind of turn them - selves into knives.
            |E                     |G♯m7
And don't    mind my nerve. You could     call it fiction,
     |F♯m7                           |A        B          |F♯
But I      like being submerged in your contradic  -  tions, dear.
       |A                |F♯          |
'Cause here      we are,
A          |E           |G♯m7         |F♯m7        |A      B
Here    we    are.
```

Verse 2

```
        ‖E                   |G♯m7
Although    you were biased, I love your advice.
      |F♯m7
Your comebacks, they're quick
                      |A              B
And probably have to do with your inse - curities.
            |E
There's no    shame in being crazy,
     |G♯m7                        |
De - pending on how you take these
F♯m7                     |A            B        ‖
Words I'm paraphrasing, this re - lationship we're    staging.
```

141

Pre-Chorus 2

```
        A                   |              |B        |          |
        And what a beautiful mess this is.
        A         |         |B        |
        It's like  picking up trash in   dresses.
```

Chorus 2

```
        ‖E                 |G♯m7                       |
        Well, it  kind of hurts when the    kind of words you say
        F♯m7              |A              B        |
        Kind of turn them - selves into blades.
        E                     |G♯m7
        Kind and courteous is     a life I've heard,
          |F♯m7                  |A          B       |F♯
        But it's     nice to say that we played in the dirt,  oh dear.
             |A              |F♯
        'Cause here      we are,
                      |A            ‖
        Here  we are.
```

Bridge

```
        E                  |G♯m7              |
          (Here we are.)        Here we are.
        F♯m7             |A         B         |
          Here  we are.    Here  we are.
        E                  |G♯m7              |
          (Here we are.       Here  we are.)
        F♯m7             |A         B            ‖
          Here  we are.    We're still here.
```

Pre-Chorus 3

    A | |B | |
And what a beautiful mess this is.

    A | |B |
It's like   taking a guess when the only answer is yes.

Chorus 3

        ||E |G♯m7
Through   timeless words and   priceless pictures

    |F♯m7 |A   B
We'll   fly like birds   not of this earth.

    |E |G♯m7
And   tides they turn, and   hearts disfigure,

    |F♯m7 |A   B
But that's   no concern when we're wounded togeth - er.

    |E |G♯m7
And we   tore our dresses and   stained our shirts,

    |F♯m7 |
But it's   nice today.

    |A   B | ||
Oh, the wait was so worth it.

Outro

    E |G♯m7 |F♯m7 |A   B |E ||

Sunshine Song

Words and Music by
Jason Mraz and Eric Hinojosa

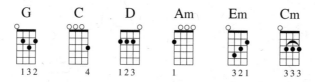

Chorus 1

‖**G**
Well, sometimes the sun shines on

|**C**
Other people's houses and not mine.

|**G**
Some days the clouds paint the sky all gray

|**D**
And it takes away my summertime.

|**G**
Somehow the sun keeps shining upon you

|**C**
While I struggle to get mine.

|**G**   **D**
If there's a light in every - body,

|**C**   **D**   **G** |**C** **D** **G**
Send out your ray of sun - shine.

Copyright © 2010 Goo Eyed Music (ASCAP), De Luz Music (ASCAP) and No BS Publishing (ASCAP)
International Copyright Secured   All Rights Reserved

Verse 1

        ‖**G**
I want to walk the same roads as everybody else,

        │**Am**
Through the trees and past the gates.

    │**C**
Getting high on heavenly breezes,

      │**C**   **D**   **G**
Making new friends a - long the way.

│**G**
I won't ask much of nobody;

      │**Am**
I'm just here to sing along,

 │**C**
And make my mistakes looks gracious,

      │**C**   **D**   **G**
And learn some lessons from my wrongs.

Chorus 2

           ‖**G**
But sometimes the sun shines on

       │**C**
Other people's houses and not mine.

       │**G**
Some days the clouds paint the sky all gray

     │**D**
And it takes away my summertime.

      │**G**
Somehow the sun keeps shining upon you

     │**C**
While I struggle to get mine.

   │**G**   **D**
A little light never hurt nobod - y;

      │**C**   **D**   **G**   │**C** **D** **G**
Send out your ray of sun - shine.

Bridge

|| **Em**
Oh, if this little light of mine

|**G**
Combined with yours today,

|**C**
How many watts could we 'luminate?

|**G**   **D**
How many villages could we save?

|**Em** |**G**
My   umbrella's tired of the weather wearing me down.

|**C** |**Cm** ||
Well, look at me now.

Interlude   **G** |**C** |**Am** |**C** **D** **G**

Verse 2

|| **G**
Well, you should look as good as your outlook.

|**Am**
Would you mind if I took some time

|**C**
To soak up your light, your beautiful light?

|**C**   **D**   **G**
You've got a para - dise in - side.

|**G**
I get hungry for love and thirsty for life,

|**Am**
And much too full on the pain,

|**C**
When I look to the sky to help me,

|**C**   **D**   **G**
And some - times it looks like rain.

Chorus 3

‖**G**
As the sun shines on

　　　|**C**
Other people's houses and not mine,

　|**G**
And the sky paints those clouds in a way

　|**D**
That it takes away the summertime,

　　|**G**
Somehow the sun keeps shining upon you

　|**C**
While I kindly stand by.

　　|**G**　　　　**D**
If there's a light in every - body,

　　　|**C**　　**D**　**G**　　　|**C D G**　　|**C D G**　　|**C D G**
Send out your ray of sun - shine.

Outro

　　　‖**G**
You're undeniably warm, you're cerulean;

　|**Am**　　　　　　|
You're perfect in design.

C　　　　　　　　|
　Won't you hang around

　|**G**　　　　　|**C**
So the sun, it can shine on　　me,

　|**G**　　　　　　|**D**
And the clouds, they can roll a - way,

　|**G**　　　　　|**C**
And the sky can become a possibility?

　　|**G**　　　**D**
If there's a light in every - body,

　　　|**C**　　**D**　**G**　　　‖
Send out your ray of sun - shine.

Anything You Want

Words and Music by
Jason Mraz and Elan Avi Atias

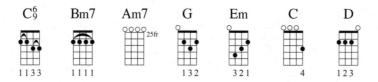

Intro

C⁶₉ | Bm7 | Am7 | |

C⁶₉ | Bm7 | Am7 | |
    Oh,   it's not for you.

C⁶₉ | Bm7
    It's what I got to give,   it's what I got to give,
| Am7 | |
It's what I got to give, it's what I got...
G   Em | G   Em | G   Em | G   Em ‖

Verse 1

G   Em | G   Em |
Courage is the triumph   of the soul.
G   Em |
I know where I wanna walk;
G   Em |
I know where I wanna go.
Am7   Bm7 | C
Come put your hand in mine;
D | G   Em | G   Em ‖
Everybody's welcome.

Copyright © 2010 Goo Eyed Music (ASCAP), WB Music Corp. (ASCAP) and Hashems Music (ASCAP)
All Rights for Hashems Music Administered by WB Music Corp.
International Copyright Secured   All Rights Reserved

Verse 2

```
        G               Em        |G     Em      |
Music is what God wants us to do.
   G                  Em
   Sing a song for me,
   |G                    Em
And I'll sing a song for you.
      |Am7       Bm7      |C
When we put our voices to - gether,
D        |G      Em   |G
We create a harmony.
```

Chorus 1

```
    Em                    ‖C                              |
And we bring you some love-a love-a love love-a love-a love,
Bm7                          |Am7
Love-a love-a love love-a love love.
              |Am7               Bm7
Yeah, you can sing if you want to.
     |C                        |
It's love-a love-a love love-a love-a love,
Bm7                   |Am7
Love-a love-a la la love.
              |Am7           |
Yeah, now we've got you.
Am7       Bm7          |C
All I want to share with you is all my love,
      D     |G     Em  |G    Em    ‖
It's all I really care to do.
```

<pre>
                G   Em |G   Em |
Verse 3   Champion the idea   of one   love.

                G   Em
                  All people the same,

                 |G   Em |Am7   Bm7 |
                One beautiful race,

                C   D |G   Em |G   Em
                   Making a home of this beautiful place.

                     |G   Em |G   Em |
                And be grateful for the pre - cious gifts of life:

                G   Em |
                   Sunshine and wa - ter,

                G   Em |
                Food from the greatest giv - er.

                Am7   Bm7 |C   D |G   Em |G   Em |
                Anything you want can be yours at any time.

                Am7   Bm7 |C   D |G   Em |G   Em ||
                Anything you want can be yours at any time.

Interlude   G   Em |G   Em |G   Em |G   Em |

                G   Em |G   Em |G   Em |G   Em
</pre>

‖**C** |

Chorus 2 It's love-a love-a love love-a love-a love,

Bm7 |**Am7** |
Love-a love-a love love-a love love.

Am7 **Bm7**
Sing out the words, sing out the words.

|**C** |
It's love-a love-a love love-a love-a love,

Bm7 |**Am7** |
Love-a love-a la la love.   Yeah,

Am7 |
  Now we know.

Am7 **Bm7** |**C**
All I want to share with you is all my love;

  D |**G** **Em** |**G** **Em**
It's all I really care to do.

‖**Am7** **Bm7** |**C** **D** |**G** **Em** |**G** **Em** |

Outro 'Cause anything you want can be yours at any time.

Am7 **Bm7** |**C**
All I want to share with you is all my love;

  D |**G** **Em** |**G** **Em** |
It's all I really care to do.

Am7 **Bm7** |**C** **D** |
Anything you want can be yours at any time.

G **Em** |**G** **Em** |**G** **Em** |
    Anything   you want,   anything   you woh...

G **Em** |**G** **Em** |**G** **Em** |**G** **Em** |**G** **Em** |
              Any - thing you want,

Am7 **Bm7** |**C** **D** | ‖
Anything you want can be yours at any time.

I Won't Give Up

Words and Music by
Jason Mraz and Michael Natter

A   E   B4   B   C#m7   Amaj7   F#m   D   D#m7b5   C#m

Intro

| A E | | A E | | |

| A E | | Bsus4 | B |

Verse 1

‖ A E |

When I look into your eyes,

| A E |

It's like watching the night   sky

| A E |

Or a beautiful sun - rise.

| Bsus4   B

Oh, there's so much they hold.

Verse 2

‖ A E |

And just like them old   stars,

| A   E |

I see that you've come so far

| A E |

To be right where you are.

| Bsus4 | B

How old is your soul?

Copyright © 2012 Goo-Eyed Music (ASCAP) and Great Hooks Music c/o NoBS Publishing (ASCAP)
International Copyright Secured   All Rights Reserved

Chorus 1

```
                   ‖A      |E
Well, I won't give up on us
          |C♯m7   |B
Even  if  the  skies  get  rough.
               |A      |E
I'm  giving  you  all  my  love.
                     |Bsus4    |B
I'm  still  looking  up.
```

Verse 3

```
                        ‖A    E   |
And  when  you're  needing  your  space
           |A      E       |
To  do  some  navigat - ing,
            |A        E      |
I'll  be  here  patiently  wait - ing
                   |Bsus4      |B
To  see  what  you  find.
```

Chorus 2

```
                   ‖A          |E
'Cause  even  the  stars,  they  burn;
          |C♯m7              |B
Some  even  fall  to  the  earth.
            |A    |E
We  got  a  lot  to  learn.
                        |Bsus4      |B
God  knows,  we're  worth        it.
                     |Amaj7     |
No,  I  won't  give  up.
```

Bridge

|F#m | |

I don't wanna be someone who walks away so easi - ly.

                                 |B   Bsus4 |B

I'm here to stay and make the difference that I can make.

  |F#m |

Our differences, they do a lot to teach us how to use

                             |B   Bsus4 |B

The tools and gifts we got; yeah, we got a lot at stake.

            |D

And in the end, you're still my friend; at least we did intend

    |D |

For us to work. We didn't break; we didn't burn.

D#m7♭5 | |

      We had to learn how to bend without the world caving in.

D |D#m7♭5   B

  I had to learn what I got,   and what I'm not

         |E |

And who I am.

Chorus 3

       ||A |E

I won't give up on us

      |C#m7 |B

Even if the skies get rough.

       |A |E

I'm giving you all my love.

        |C#m7

I'm still looking up.

      |Bsus4

I'm still looking up.

Chorus 4

<pre>
         ‖A |E
Well, I won't give up (No, I'm not) on us. (giving up.)
           |C♯m7 |B
God knows, I'm tough (I am tough.) e - nough. (I am loved.)
          |A |E
We've got a lot (We're alive.) to learn. (We are loved.)
                  |B   Bsus4 |B
God knows, we're worth it. (And we're worth it.)
</pre>

Outro

<pre>
          ‖A |E
I won't give up on us.
               |C♯m |B
Even if the skies get rough.
             |A |E
I'm giving you all my love.

                 |B   ‖
I'm still looking up.
</pre>

More Great Piano/Vocal Books

FROM CHERRY LANE

For a complete listing of Cherry Lane titles available,
including contents listings, please visit our web site at
www.cherrylane.com

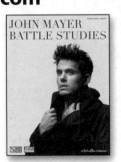

02501590	Sara Bareilles – Kaleidoscope Heart	$17.99
02501136	Sara Bareilles – Little Voice	$16.95
02501505	The Black Eyed Peas – The E.N.D.	$19.99
02502171	The Best of Boston	$17.95
02501123	Buffy the Vampire Slayer – Once More with Feeling	$18.95
02500665	Sammy Cahn Songbook	$24.95
02501454	Colbie Caillat – Breakthrough	$17.99
02501127	Colbie Caillat – Coco	$16.95
02500144	Mary Chapin Carpenter – Party Doll & Other Favorites	$16.95
02502165	John Denver Anthology – Revised	$22.95
02500002	John Denver Christmas	$14.95
02502166	John Denver's Greatest Hits	$17.95
02502151	John Denver – A Legacy in Song (Softcover)	$24.95
02502152	John Denver – A Legacy in Song (Hardcover)	$34.95
02500566	Poems, Prayers and Promises: The Art and Soul of John Denver	$19.95
02500326	John Denver – The Wildlife Concert	$17.95
02500501	John Denver and the Muppets: A Christmas Together	$9.95
02501186	The Dresden Dolls – The Virginia Companion	$39.95
02509922	The Songs of Bob Dylan	$29.95
02500497	Linda Eder – Gold	$14.95
02500396	Linda Eder – Christmas Stays the Same	$17.95
02500175	Linda Eder – It's No Secret Anymore	$14.95
02502209	Linda Eder – It's Time	$17.95
02500630	Donald Fagen – 5 of the Best	$7.95
02501542	Foreigner – The Collection	$19.99
02500535	Erroll Garner Anthology	$19.95
02500318	Gladiator	$12.95
02502126	Best of Guns N' Roses	$17.95
02502072	Guns N' Roses – Selections from Use Your Illusion I and II	$17.95
02500014	Sir Roland Hanna Collection	$19.95
02500856	Jack Johnson – Anthology	$19.95
02501140	Jack Johnson – Sleep Through the Static	$16.95
02501564	Jack Johnson – To the Sea	$19.99
02501546	Jack's Mannequin – The Glass Passenger and The Dear Jack EP	$19.99
02500381	Lenny Kravitz – Greatest Hits	$14.95
02501318	John Legend – Evolver	$19.99
02503701	Man of La Mancha	$11.95
02501047	Dave Matthews Band – Anthology	$24.95
02500693	Dave Matthews – Some Devil	$16.95
02502192	Dave Matthews Band – Under the Table and Dreaming	$17.95
02501514	John Mayer Anthology – Volume 1	$22.99
02501504	John Mayer – Battle Studies	$19.99
02500987	John Mayer – Continuum	$16.95
02500681	John Mayer – Heavier Things	$16.95
02500563	John Mayer – Room for Squares	$16.95
02500081	Natalie Merchant – Ophelia	$14.95
02500863	Jason Mraz – Mr. A-Z	$17.95
02501467	Jason Mraz – We Sing. We Dance. We Steal Things.	$19.99
02502895	Nine	$17.95
02501411	Nine – Film Selections	$19.99
02500425	Time and Love: The Art and Soul of Laura Nyro	$21.95
02502204	The Best of Metallica	$17.95
02501497	Ingrid Michaelson – Everybody	$17.99
02501496	Ingrid Michaelson – Girls and Boys	$19.99
02501529	Monte Montgomery Collection	$24.99
02501336	Amanda Palmer – Who Killed Amanda Palmer?	$17.99
02501004	Best of Gram Parsons	$16.95
02501137	Tom Paxton – Comedians & Angels	$16.95
02500010	Tom Paxton – The Honor of Your Company	$17.95
02507962	Peter, Paul & Mary – Holiday Concert	$17.95
02500145	Pokemon 2.B.A. Master	$12.95
02500026	The Prince of Egypt	$16.95
02500660	Best of Bonnie Raitt	$17.95
02502189	The Bonnie Raitt Collection	$22.95
02502088	Bonnie Raitt – Luck of the Draw	$14.95
02507958	Bonnie Raitt – Nick of Time	$14.95
02502218	Kenny Rogers – The Gift	$16.95
02501577	She & Him – Volume One	$16.99
02501578	She & Him – Volume Two	$17.99
02500414	Shrek	$16.99
02500536	Spirit – Stallion of the Cimarron	$16.95
02500166	Steely Dan – Anthology	$17.95
02500622	Steely Dan – Everything Must Go	$14.95
02500284	Steely Dan – Two Against Nature	$14.95
02500344	Billy Strayhorn: An American Master	$17.95
02500515	Barbra Streisand – Christmas Memories	$16.95
02507969	Barbra Streisand – A Collection: Greatest Hits and More	$17.95
02502164	Barbra Streisand – The Concert	$22.95
02500550	Essential Barbra Streisand	$24.95
02502228	Barbra Streisand – Higher Ground	$17.99
02501065	Barbra Streisand – Live in Concert 2006	$19.95
02501485	Barbra Streisand – Love Is the Answer	$19.99
02503617	John Tesh – Avalon	$15.95
02502178	The John Tesh Collection	$17.95
02503623	John Tesh – A Family Christmas	$15.95
02503630	John Tesh – Grand Passion	$16.95
02500307	John Tesh – Pure Movies 2	$16.95
02501068	The Evolution of Robin Thicke	$19.95
02500565	Thoroughly Modern Millie	$17.99
02501399	Best of Toto	$19.99
02502175	Tower of Power – Silver Anniversary	$17.95
02501403	Keith Urban – Defying Gravity	$17.99
02501008	Keith Urban – Love, Pain & The Whole Crazy Thing	$17.95
02501141	Keith Urban – Greatest Hits	$16.99
02502198	The "Weird Al" Yankovic Anthology	$17.95
02500334	Maury Yeston – December Songs	$17.95
02502225	The Maury Yeston Songbook	$19.95

See your local music dealer or contact:

7777 W. BLUEMOUND RD. P.O. BOX 13819 MILWAUKEE, WI 53213

Prices, contents and availability subject to change without notice.

0811